A DANGEROUS WOMAN

A Dangerous Woman

The Graphic Biography of Emma Goldman

Written and Picturized by
Sharon Rudahl
Edited by Paul Buhle

THE NEW PRESS
NEW YORK
LONDON

Published in the United States by The New Press, New York, 2007. Distributed by Perseus Distribution

LIBRARY OF CONGRESS CATALOGING-IN-PUBLICATION DATA
Rudahl, Sharon.
A dangerous woman : the graphic biography of Emma Goldman / written and picturized by Sharon Rudahl ; edited by Paule Buhle.
p. cm.
ISBN 978-1-59558-064-1 (pbk)
1. Goldman, Emma, 1869-1940--Comic books, strips, etc. 2. Anarchists--United States--Biography--Comic books, strips, etc. I. Buhle, Paul, 1944- II. Title.
HX843.7.G65R83 2007
335'.83092--dc22
[B]

2007015415

The New Press publishes books that promote and enrich public discussion and understanding of the issues vital to our democracy and to a more equitable world. These books are made possible by the enthusiasm of our readers; the support of a committed group of donors, large and small; the collaboration of our many partners in the independent media and the not-for-profit sector; booksellers, who often hand-sell New Press books; librarians; and above all by our authors.

www.thenewpress.com

Printed in the United States of America

~ DEDICATED TO ALL THE DANGEROUS PEOPLE ~ PASSING AND TO COME ~

AND TO MY PARENTS ~ NORMAN AND RUTH KAHN

MY MOTHER DIED PEACEFULLY IN ADVANCED AGE AS I WAS WRITING THE LAST CHAPTER OF THIS BOOK AND MY FATHER ONE AND A HALF YEARS LATER, SHORTLY BEFORE I FINISHED DRAWING IT.

AS THEY CHOSE NOT TO HAVE GRAVES, LET THESE PAGES SERVE AS THEIR MEMORIAL.

SHARON RUDAHL

CONTENTS

FOREWORD ix

TERRIBLE CHILD. 2

A NEW WORLD 12

THE STRONGEST LINK 22

BLACKWELL'S ISLAND 33

RED EMMA. 39

FIREBRAND 50

FROM MISS SMITH TO MOTHER EARTH 58

KING OF THE HOBOS 69

LOVE AND WAR 81

EXILE TO EXILE 90

TO THE BARRICADES 99

AUTHOR'S NOTE 113

FOREWORD

WHY EMMA GOLDMAN?

Of all the radicals in the early twentieth century United States, the Russian-born anarchist Emma Goldman entered most deeply into the popular imagination. To her critics, she was "the most dangerous woman in America," an advocate of free love and bombs. To her admirers, she was the bravest and truest of revolutionaries, the most "modern" of the twentieth century's "new women." She remains an icon of resistance to injustice, the emblem of a woman who never gave up or gave in.

She embraced anarchism in the aftermath of the Haymarket affair of 1886, when four Chicago-based anarchists were executed following a bomb explosion in Haymarket Square. The speeches of the accused men, and the obvious injustice of the trial, galvanized Goldman into political activism. She soon developed her own idiosyncratic vision, melding the anarchism of her beloved Russian mentors Michael Bakunin and Peter Kropotkin with the American individualism of Walt Whitman, the sexual radicalism of the "free lovers," and the modernism of the bohemian avant-garde. For more than twenty years she made annual cross-country lecture tours, addressing thousands of Americans for whom her courage and outspokenness served as a model of anarchism in action. While she converted few to her belief in direct action and the evils of the capitalist state, she persuaded many more of the value of free speech and of emancipation from internal as well as external tyrants. She wasn't afraid to go to jail and served several prison terms, including two long years for her opposition to World War I.

Flouting all the old Victorian pieties, Emma Goldman also embodied the twentieth century's "new woman." She took lovers, dispensed birth control information in her lectures, and insisted that anarchist ideas of individuality and freedom applied to women as well as to men. Her more conventional comrades bristled at her feminism, although she disliked that word. They chided her for broaching "unnatural" subjects such as homosexuality and for reaching out to middle-class intellectuals and artists. She replied that sexuality was also political and that art, especially the theater, could change people's lives. And besides, she was reaching far more people with her progressive vision than those who remained in their tiny enclaves of the converted.

She has continued to speak ever since. Google Emma Goldman on the Internet, and a host of intelligent websites come up explaining the history, philosophy, and politics of anarchism, and of Emma Goldman in particular. (In truth, I expected to see bombs and dynamite, those worn old stereotypes of anarchy that still surface from time to time in the daily press.) Hear the echoes of Emma Goldman in the student demonstrations of 1968, in the feminist collectives of the 1970s and 1980s, in the antiglobalization protests of the 1990s and after.

Here's another surprise. Open this book, and you will enter almost physically into the everyday world of Goldman, through Sharon Rudahl's captivating graphic images. Rudahl beautifully conveys the drama of Goldman's life through her imaginative, meticulous drawings that open up entire worlds, from the streets of Czarist St. Petersburg to the slums and prisons of turn-of-the-century New York, the devastated towns of the Ukraine during the Civil War, and the rural collectives of anarchist Spain. Both activist and artist, Rudahl brings to her graphic art a visceral understanding of the life of a revolutionary as well as an artist's eye for the compelling incident and image.

But why Emma Goldman today? Surely in a world of global corporate capitalism, almost permanent war, global warming, and a growing gulf between rich and poor—within as well as between nations—Goldman's anarchist ideal of society without the state seems farther away than in her own time. Yet in other respects, Goldman's inclusive vision, her way of being in the world, strikes a more powerful chord than ever. How much we need her skill at bringing people of diverse backgrounds together, her conviction that difference enriches human connection and possibility. How resonant is her opposition to unjust war, her claim that patriotism means loving our country with open eyes. How relevant today is her insistence on the dignity and worth of every human being, her empathy with the oppressed and forgotten, her refusal to give up the struggle for justice, no matter how grim the circumstances that confronted her.

And how fitting for one who believed deeply in the power of art to transform lives that her biography now comes to us through graphic images. In the pages of this book we see her vivid and alive. These are not in the haunted still photographs taken by the police or by prison or immigration officials for the purpose of identification and incarceration. Nor are they images from the new technology of the newsreel, which captured a defiant Goldman in December 1919 as she boarded the SS *Buford* with 247 other immigrant deportees kicked out of the United States at the height of the post–World War I Red Scare. Compelling as such images are, they document limited moments in Goldman's biography, usually those of heightened surveillance. Rudahl goes beyond such moments to give us the full measure of Goldman as she traversed the great events of the nineteenth and twentieth centuries. In a powerful dance of image and text that matches the energy and originality of her subject, Sharon Rudahl honors Emma Goldman's life.

—Alice Wexler

A DANGEROUS WOMAN

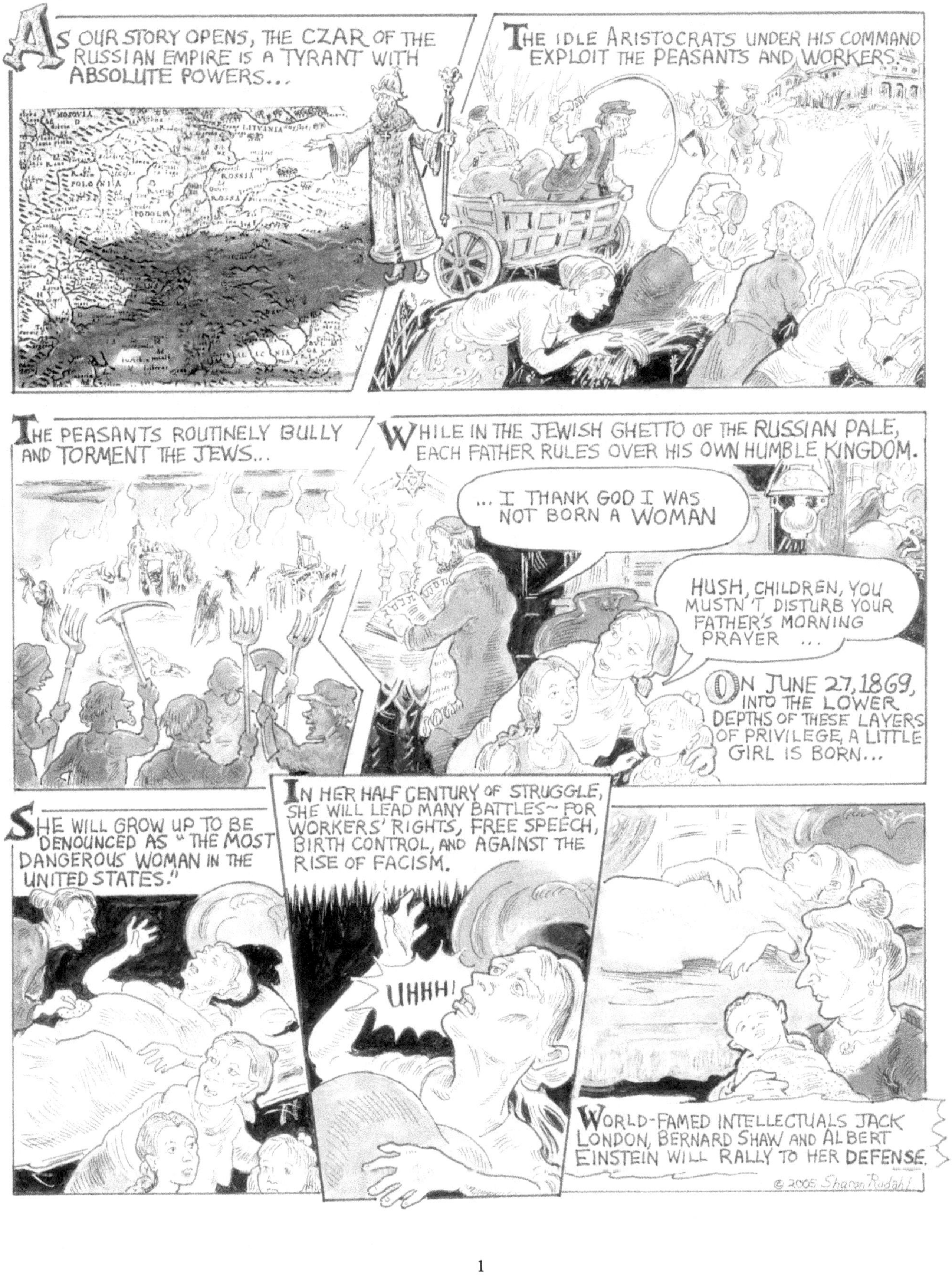

THE PEASANTS ROUTINELY BULLY AND TORMENT THE JEWS...

WHILE IN THE JEWISH GHETTO OF THE RUSSIAN PALE, EACH FATHER RULES OVER HIS OWN HUMBLE KINGDOM.

... I THANK GOD I WAS NOT BORN A WOMAN

HUSH, CHILDREN, YOU MUSTN'T DISTURB YOUR FATHER'S MORNING PRAYER ...

ON JUNE 27, 1869, INTO THE LOWER DEPTHS OF THESE LAYERS OF PRIVILEGE, A LITTLE GIRL IS BORN...

SHE WILL GROW UP TO BE DENOUNCED AS "THE MOST DANGEROUS WOMAN IN THE UNITED STATES."

IN HER HALF CENTURY OF STRUGGLE, SHE WILL LEAD MANY BATTLES~ FOR WORKERS' RIGHTS, FREE SPEECH, BIRTH CONTROL, AND AGAINST THE RISE OF FACISM.

UHHH!

WORLD-FAMED INTELLECTUALS JACK LONDON, BERNARD SHAW AND ALBERT EINSTEIN WILL RALLY TO HER DEFENSE.

VICTORIOUS REVOLUTIONARIES WILL HONOR HER. THE DAUGHTERS OF PLUTOCRATS WILL FUND HER LAST EXILE ON THE CÔTE D'AZUR. SHE WILL ENTRANCE COUNTLESS LOVERS, AND ALWAYS REMAIN FAITHFUL TO ONE LIFETIME UNION~
HER NAME IS EMMA GOLDMAN
FEH! NOT ANOTHER GIRL!!
TERRIBLE CHILD
HER FATHER ABRAHAM WAS HARSH AND BITTER,
HER MOTHER TAUBE COLD & PREOCCUPIED.
LENA, SEVEN YEARS OLDER, INEXPLICABLY JEALOUS & CRUEL.
ONLY THE OLDEST SISTER~ TIMID, SELF-SACRIFICING HELENA~PROTECTED & CONSOLED LITTLE EMMA.
©Sharon Rudahl 2005
UNDER RUSSIAN RULE, JEWS COULD NOT OWN LAND, & WERE BARRED FROM MOST OCCUPATIONS. EMMA'S FATHER MANAGED THE STAGECOACH INN AT POPELAN, NEAR LATVIA.
EMMA NEVER FORGOT SEEING PEASANT BOYS FORCIBLY CONSCRIPTED INTO THE CZAR'S ARMY...
HEARTBROKEN MOTHERS TORE THEIR HAIR, BEAT THEIR BREASTS AND FILLED THE AIR WITH THEIR PLAINTS...

WHEN EMMA WAS FOUR, BROTHER HERMAN WAS BORN, & TWO YEARS LATER YEGOR "REPLACED THE NEED FOR DOLLS IN MY LIFE."
EMMA EVEN TRIED NURSING YEGOR AT HER OWN BREAST.
THE BABY'S CHOKING!!
UHHGH, UHH, UHHGGHH~
AT ANY INFRACTION, ABRAHAM TOOK OUT HIS STRAP...
I WILL KILL THAT BRAT! I WILL TEACH HER TO OBEY!!
YEEEOOW!
WHAP
WHAP
WHAP!
© Sharon Rudahl 2005
AND ALWAYS HELENA COMFORTED EMMA AND BATHED HER WOUNDS...
WHEN LENA CONDESCENDED TO PLAY WITH EMMA, SHE EXPECTED TO WIN EVERY TIME...
CHEATER! JUST LIKE YOUR FATHER... HE ROBBED US OF THE MONEY OUR FATHER LEFT FOR US!
I HATE YOU! YOU ARE NOT MY REAL SISTER!

IT'S TIME YOU KNEW... LENA & HELENA'S FATHER WAS MY FIRST HUSBAND...
TAUBE HAD BEEN LEFT A WIDOW WITH TWO YOUNG DAUGHTERS, HER 2ND MARRIAGE ARRANGED TO THE MUCH YOUNGER, POORER ABRAHAM.
YOUR FATHER INVESTED DR. ZODIKOW'S MONEY FOR THE GOOD OF OUR WHOLE FAMILY... IT'S NO ONE'S FAULT THE BUSINESS FAILED...
LEFT TO RUN WILD, THE LONELY LITTLE GIRL SAW & JUDGED.
SPARE A KOPEK FOR A WOUNDED SOLDIER, MISSY?
GO JUMP IN THE RIVER, THEN~ THERE'S NO PLACE HERE FOR YOUR BASTARD!
IF I HAD NOT BEEN BORN WITH LOVE FOR FREEDOM AND INTENSE HATRED OF INJUSTICE, I DO NOT BELIEVE I WOULD HAVE BECOME WHAT I AM...
EMMA WAS HAPPIEST WHEN THE YOUNG SHEPHERD PETRUSHA TOOK HER TO THE MEADOWS...
HE WOULD CARRY HER HOME ON HIS SHOULDERS
AND GRATEFUL EMMA STOLE CAKE AND JAM FROM TAUBE'S PANTRY FOR HIM.
SOON ENOUGH, ABRAHAM SENT PETRUSHA PACKING...
I WON'T TOLERATE A THIEF!
I MEANT NO HARM, SIR...

EMMA LONGED FOR HIM...
IF I EVER FIND YOUR HAND LIKE THAT AGAIN, I'LL WHIP YOU, YOU NAUGHTY GIRL!!
WHEN EMMA WAS 8, SHE WAS SENT TO LIVE WITH HER GRANDMOTHER AND UNCLE IN KÖNIGSBERG. THERE SHE COULD ATTEND A JEWISH DAY SCHOOL.
HERE'S 40 KOPEKS FOR HER BOARD AND SCHOOL FEES~ I'LL SEND ANOTHER 40 EVERY MONTH...
BUT WHILE GRANDMA WENT AWAY TO PLY HER TRADE AS A SMUGGLER, EMMA'S UNCLE POCKETED THE HARD-EARNED KOPEKS. EMMA WAS FORCED TO WORK AS A MAID...
© Sharon Rudahl
EACH MONTH, HE SENT FAKE SCHOOL REPORTS TO EMMA'S PARENTS.
HURRY AND BOIL THESE SHEETS!
I'M NOT YOUR SERVANT!!
MEIN GOTT!

THE KINDLY OLD MAIDS DOWNSTAIRS CONTACTED EMMA'S FAMILY IN POPELAN, & HER FATHER CAME TO TAKE HER HOME...

GENTLY, NOW

WHEN ABRAHAM SAW EMMA ~ THIN, BATTERED, DRESSED IN RAGS

HE EMBRACED HIS DAUGHTER FOR THE 1ST TIME IN FOUR YEARS...

BACK IN POPELAN, ABRAHAM LOST HIS POST AS MANAGER OF THE INN.

BECAUSE WE ARE **JEWS** ~ AND THE OTHER MAN GAVE MORE **VODKA**...

HELENA BID FAREWELL TO HER ONE FRIEND, A LITHUANIAN CHRISTIAN.

LOVE BETWEEN JEW AND GENTILE WAS CONSIDERED THE CRIME OF CRIMES.

THE ENTIRE FAMILY MOVED TO KÖNIGSBERG, AND EMMA WAS FINALLY ENROLLED IN PRIMARY SCHOOL.

I CAN ARRANGE SCHOLARSHIPS FOR EMMA AND HERMAN... BUT I'LL NEED TO SEE MONTHLY PROGRESS REPORTS!!

"THE REGIME WAS **HARSH**, THE INSTRUCTORS **BRUTAL**."
WHACK!
WH
WHACK!!

EMMA BECAME RINGLEADER OF A GROUP THAT TORMENTED THE RELIGION TEACHER ~ PUTTING **TACKS** ON HIS CHAIR OR **KNOTTING** HIS COATTAILS...

THE GEOGRAPHY TEACHER KEPT A DIFFERENT GIRL **AFTER HOURS** EVERY DAY...

AH, MISS GOLDMAN, OUR NEW PUPIL... I'M SURE **YOU** WANT TO PLEASE YOUR TEACHER...

©SHARON RUDAHL 2005

School was not all hard times...the consumptive German teacher befriended Emma, introducing her to MUSIC and POETRY.
"Oh friends! Not these gloomy sounds! Let us rather sing more pleasing and joyful ones!"
Goethe
Schiller
She took Emma out to the OPERA~the sensitive girl's first taste of theatrical magic...
A FAIRYLAND more magnificent than any ever pictured in the stories I had read...
© Sharon Rudahl '07
When Emma was 12, Czar Alexander II was assassinated by young revolutionaries. All suspected radicals were arrested, including Taube's kid brother in St. Petersburg.
DEATH of CZAR ALEXANDER II MURDERED REPORT ALL SUSPICIOUS PERSONS
OUR GRACIOUS CZAR! THOSE COLD-BLOODED NIHILISTS!!
Abraham was offered a job as manager of his cousin's dry goods store in St. Petersburg.
I WON'T GO! I CAN STAY WITH MY GERMAN TEACHER~
I WANT TO STUDY MEDICINE, SO I CAN BE USEFUL IN THE WORLD!
GIRLS DO NOT HAVE TO LEARN MUCH!!
ALL A JEWISH DAUGHTER NEEDS TO KNOW IS HOW TO PREPARE GEFILTE FISH, CUT NOODLES FINE, AND GIVE THE MAN PLENTY OF CHILDREN!
But after ceaseless pleading, Emma's parents agreed to let her stay~ IF she could pass the entrance exam for Gymnasium...
ALGEB

EMMA PASSED HER EXAM... THE FINAL REQUIREMENT WAS A "CERTIFICATE OF GOOD CHARACTER," FROM HER RELIGION TEACHER...
PLEASE, SIR~ FOR MY APPLICATION TO GYMNASIUM~
I WILL NEVER GIVE YOU A "GOOD CHARACTER"!! YOU ARE A TERRIBLE CHILD AND WILL GROW INTO A WORSE WOMAN!
YOU HAVE NO RESPECT FOR YOUR ELDERS OR FOR AUTHORITY! YOU WILL SURELY END ON THE GALLOWS AS A PUBLIC MENACE!!
WHEN ABRAHAM REACHED ST. PETERSBURG, HIS COUSIN'S STORE HAD ALREADY GONE OUT OF BUSINESS. TAUBE AND THE CHILDREN PAID TO BE SMUGGLED ACROSS THE FROZEN BORDER MARSHES TO JOIN HIM.
SILENCE, OR THE GUARDS WILL OPEN FIRE!
EMMA HAD BEEN PROMISED A CHANCE TO STUDY IN ST. PETERSBURG... INSTEAD, SHE HAD TO JOIN HER SISTERS, WORKING TO SUPPORT THE FAMILY... FIRST, KNITTING SHAWLS AT HOME-
NEXT, AT A GLOVE FACTORY-
THE GIRLS TALKED AND SANG, & WERE ALLOWED TEA BREAKS. BUT THE HOURS WERE LONG, THE WORK GRUELING, AND THE PAY MEAGER...
A PITY WE WILL NEVER WEAR SUCH LOVELY THINGS!!

ST. PETERSBURG IN THE 1880S WAS A GRAND CAPITAL CITY, HOME TO THE RICHEST, MOST WORLDLY JEWISH COMMUNITY IN RUSSIA. HELENA'S BOSS ONCE GAVE HER TWO TICKETS TO A BALL AT THE FASHIONABLE GERMAN CLUB...
THERE'S A LENGTH OF BLUE VELVETEEN I COULD BRING HOME TO MAKE YOUR GOWN~
BUT I'M AFRAID FATHER WILL REFUSE TO LET US GO...
THEN I WILL DEFY HIM!!
THE NIGHT OF THE BALL~ EMMA WAITED FOR HER PARENTS TO FALL ASLEEP.
WAKE UP, HELENA! IF YOU WON'T COME WITH ME, I'LL RUN OFF BY MYSELF!
WE CAN BE BACK BEFORE FATHER WAKES UP!!
EMMA WAS ASKED FOR EVERY DANCE...
IT'S GETTING LATE- WE HAVE TO GO HOME!!
I WILL DANCE!
I WILL DANCE MYSELF TO DEATH!
THE GIRLS CREPT IN AT DAWN WITHOUT WAKING THEIR PARENTS...
BUT ABRAHAM WORRIED ABOUT HIS LIVELY YOUNG DAUGHTERS... HE FOLLOWED EMMA AND HELENA TO THE SUMMER GARDENS, AND CAUGHT THEM FLIRTING WITH UPPER CLASS STUDENTS
CRACK
I WILL NOT TOLERATE A LOOSE DAUGHTER!

ST. PETERSBURG WAS A HOTBED OF DISSENT. SECRET READING CIRCLES PASSED FORBIDDEN BOOKS. HELENA'S STUDENT FRIENDS INTRODUCED HER TO THE THRILLING NEW IDEAS.
OH, EMMA, YOU MUST READ THIS!... VERA DOESN'T MARRY, SHE SIMPLY LIVES WITH THE MAN SHE LOVES... SHE DOESN'T SLAVE FOR A BOSS, SHE FORMS A CO-OP WITH HER FRIENDS!!
WHAT IS TO BE DONE
OUTSIDE THE GLOVE FACTORY, YOUNG MEN WAITED TO MEET THE WORKING GIRLS...
GIVE US A SMILE, DARLING!
I'LL SHOW YOU A GOOD TIME, TONITE!
EMMA TRIED TO RESIST...
WOULD THE LOVELY LADY PERMIT ME TO BUY HER A CUP OF COFFEE?...
EMMA AND THE HOTEL CLERK BEGAN TO MEET REGULARLY AT A NEARBY PASTRY SHOP...
I'M OFF DUTY THIS EVENING— WHY DON'T I GIVE YOU A TOUR OF THE HOTEL GRANDE?
EMMA HAD LONG IMAGINED THE JOY AND GAIETY BEHIND THE HOTEL WINDOWS.
SHE ALLOWED HERSELF TO BE LED THROUGH A SIDE ENTRANCE...
THE BEST FRENCH WINE FOR MY BEST GIRL!
I FELT NO SHAME, ONLY A GREAT SHOCK... THAT THE CONTACT BETWEEN A MAN AND A WOMAN COULD BE SO BRUTAL...

AFTER THE ASSASSINATION OF CZAR ALEXANDER II IN 1881, MODEST REFORMS FOR JEWS WERE **ANNULLED.** JEWISH SCHOOLS WERE CLOSED, YIDDISH PUBLICATIONS CENSORED, JEWS TARGETED FOR GOVERNMENT REPRISALS...

OVER THE NEXT THREE DECADES, 1/3 OF RUSSIAN JEWS **EMIGRATED,** MOST TO AMERICA. LENA LEFT FIRST, SEIZING A CHANCE TO TRAVEL AS A DOMESTIC SERVANT~

THEN HELENA MADE **HER** PLANS...

WHO **KNEW** SHE HAD SAVED ENOUGH FOR A TICKET?!

WITH YOUR SISTERS BOTH GONE, **YOU'LL** NEED TO BE SETTLED, EMMA...

THE MATCHMAKER **ASSURES** US SHE CAN FIND SOMEONE **SUITABLE**!

I'M ONLY **FIFTEEN**!!

I WANT TO **KNOW** LIFE! I WANT TO STUDY MEDICINE. I WANT TO **TRAVEL**!

IF YOU DON'T LET ME GO TO AMERICA WITH HELENA, I WILL THROW MYSELF IN THE **RIVER**!!!

IN THE LATE 19TH CENTURY, THE U.S. WAS TRANSFORMED BY A STORM SURGE OF IMMIGRATION, DARKER-SKINNED **ALIENS** FLEEING PERSECUTION, HUNGER AND UNREST. BUSINESS **FLOURISHED** WITH CHEAP LABOR, THE **OWNERSHIP** CLASS SHAMELESSLY SCRAMBLED OVER THE BACKS OF THE POOR. IT WAS THE **BEST** OF TIMES, IT WAS THE **WORST** OF TIMES, A TIME MUCH LIKE OUR OWN...

TRAVELING STEERAGE, EMMA AND HELENA REACHED NEW YORK IN DECEMBER 1885 ~ TEN MONTHS BEFORE THE OFFICIAL OPENING OF THE STATUE OF LIBERTY
SHE HOLDS HER TORCH HIGH TO LIGHT THE WAY TO THE FREE COUNTRY
AT THE CASTLE GARDEN IMMIGRATION CENTER ~
ANGRY MEN, HYSTERICAL WOMEN... GUARDS PUSHED US ROUGHLY HITHER AND THITHER. THE FIRST DAY ON AMERICAN SOIL PROVED A VIOLENT SHOCK.
THE SISTERS PROCEEDED UPSTATE TO ROCHESTER, TO JOIN LENA AND HER TINSMITH HUSBAND.
I'M SO GLAD YOU'LL BE HERE TO HELP WHEN BABY IS BORN!
THERE'S ROOM FOR YOUR SISTERS, BUT I CAN'T AFFORD TO FEED THEM FOR LONG...
YOU CAN DO WELL IN AMERICA, IF YOU'RE NOT AFRAID OF HARD WORK!
ALL MY SIX KIDS SELL NEWSPAPERS OR SHINE SHOES!
I CAN GET HER A JOB AT GARSON'S... THE WAGES ARE LOW, BUT SHE'LL SOON FIND A FELLER TO MARRY HER!
WEALTHY GERMAN JEW GARSON RAN A BETTER LIT, MORE MODERN FACTORY THAN THOSE IN PETERSBURG. BUT HIS FOREMEN WERE SLAVE DRIVERS.
PLEASE, SIR, MAY I GO TO THE TOILET?
YOU WENT THIS MORNING, HOLD IT TILL THE END OF SHIFT!
©Sharon Rudahl 2005
EMMA SEWED HEAVY OVERCOATS, 10½ HOURS A DAY, FOR $2.50 A WEEK, PAYING $1.50 TO LENA'S HUSBAND FOR BOARD.
TANYA! WHAT'S THE MATTER? ARE YOU SICK?
BACK TO YOUR MACHINES, GIRLS! DO YOU WANT TO BE FIRED?!!
I'LL GET TANYA HOME— YOU CAN DEDUCT THE TIME FROM MY PAY...
YOU CAN GO TO HELL, YOU WILDCAT!

EMMA'S NEXT JOB WAS AT RUBENSTEIN'S, FOR $4 A WEEK. SHE WORKED NEXT TO JACOB KERSNER, A LITERATE OLDER TAILOR...
THANKS SO MUCH FOR LENDING ME THE BOOK, JACOB!
WOULD YOU CONSIDER COMING TO A DANCE WITH ME, EMMA?
CRIME AND PUNISHMENT
HER FIRST DANCE IN AMERICA WAS DISAPPOINTING. JACOB GAVE UP AFTER THE FIRST FEW TUNES...
THE MUSIC SHRILL, THE DANCERS CLUMSY, THE HALL DARK AND UGLY...
FIVE YEARS AT THE MACHINES HAVE TAKEN THE STRENGTH OUT OF ME...
WITH LENA'S BABY GIRL CAME NEW EXPENSES & OBLIGATIONS.
BUT FROM HER FIRST DAYS, STELLA WAS EMMA'S DARLING~
SOON, THE REST OF THE FAMILY JOINED THE SISTERS, FLEEING FIERCE POGROMS STIRRED UP AGAINST THE JEWS.
TOO MANY MOUTHS TO FEED!!
MY WORKMATE JACOB KERSNER NEEDS A PLACE TO BOARD—AND HE'S WILLING TO PAY WELL...
OH, I DON'T LIKE HIM, EMMA!!
SEVEN ADULTS, 2 BOYS AND A BABY IN ONE SMALL HOUSE~EMMA WAS WORN OUT BY CONSTANT NOISE AND BICKERING...
BEGGARS CAN'T BE CHOOSERS! HE CAN SHARE THE LUMBER ROOM WITH HERMANN!
LET ME TAKE CARE OF YOU, EMMA—WE CAN GET A PLACE OF OUR OWN
BEFORE EMMA MARRIED JACOB KERSNER, SHE ALREADY FOUND HIM COMMONPLACE...
NOW, THE BRIDEGROOM BREAKS THE WINEGLASS, SYMBOLIZING THE DESTRUCTION OF OUR ANCIENT TABERNACLE.
ON THEIR WEDDING NIGHT, JACOB WAS IMPOTENT.

THE DOCTOR ADVISED REST, "TO BUILD UP JACOB'S MANHOOD." HE BECAME PEEVISH AND DEMANDING...
I DON'T WANT YOU GOING BACK TO THAT FACTORY! IT'S A DISGRACE FOR MY WIFE TO WORK NEXT TO SINGLE MEN!
YOU THROW AWAY ALL YOUR WAGES PLAYING CARDS!
EMMA LEFT, FINDING WORK AT A CORSET FACTORY IN NEW HAVEN. SHE FELL ILL, AND HAD TO RETURN...
WHEN SHE SUGGESTED SEPARATING, KERSNER BECAME DESPERATE.
IF YOU LEAVE AGAIN, I'LL KILL MYSELF!!
EMMA WAS TRAPPED. WHAT HAD BECOME OF HER GIRLHOOD DREAMS?
HER ONLY JOYS WERE BABY STELLA...
AND ATTENDING SOCIALIST CLUB MEETINGS WITH HELENA ~
'FREIHEIT' IS AN ANARCHIST PAPER- JOHANN MOST PUBLISHES IT IN NEW YORK CITY...
ANARCHISTS FIGHT THE BOSSES, SAME AS US - BUT THEY OPPOSE ANY KIND OF CENTRALIZED GOVERNMENT.
FREIHEIT
HAYMARKET
STRIKE
ARRESTS
© Sharon Rudahl 2005
WHAT'S ALL THIS FUSS ABOUT "HAYMARKET"?
IN CHICAGO, HAYMARKET SQUARE...
THE McCORMICK REAPER WORKERS WENT ON STRIKE TO WORK 8 HOURS A DAY, INSTEAD OF BEFORE DAWN TO AFTER DARK...
POLICE AND HIRED PINKERTON GUARDS BEAT UP THE STRIKERS- BEAT TWO OF 'EM TO DEATH!
8 HOUR DAY
ON STRIKE
ON STRIKE
JOIN US

SO THE STRIKERS CALLED A BIG PROTEST MEETING AT HAYMARKET SQUARE...
A BOMB WENT OFF— NO ONE KNOWS WHO THREW IT—
AND SEVEN POLICE WERE KILLED!!
THE CHICAGO COPS WENT CRAZY, ROUNDING UP EVERY SOCIAL ACTIVIST, TORTURING THEM...
THEY PINNED THE BOMBING ON ALBERT PARSONS, AUGUST SPIES, ADOLPH FISCHER, AND GEORGE ENGEL~ THEY WRITE FOR ANARCHIST PAPERS, BUT ONLY TWO WERE EVEN AT THE HAYMARKET MEETING.
BUT THEY'RE ALL GOING TO BE HANGED!!
EMMA SENT FOR THE ANARCHIST LITERATURE ADVERTISED IN DIE FREIHEIT... FACTORING OUT CONTRADICTIONS AND LONG-FORGOTTON SQUABBLES, HER CONCEPT OF ANARCHISM WAS AN INTOXICATING VISION OF PERFECT JUSTICE AND FREEDOM...
PYOTYR KROPOTKIN
MIKHAIL BAKUNIN
GOD AND THE STATE
PIERRE PROUDHON
IMAGINE!! NO KINGS, NO GODS, NO HUNGER OR GREED... NO REASON TO FIGHT WARS! ALL PEOPLE LIVING AS BROTHERS AND SISTERS!
©Sharon Rudahl '06

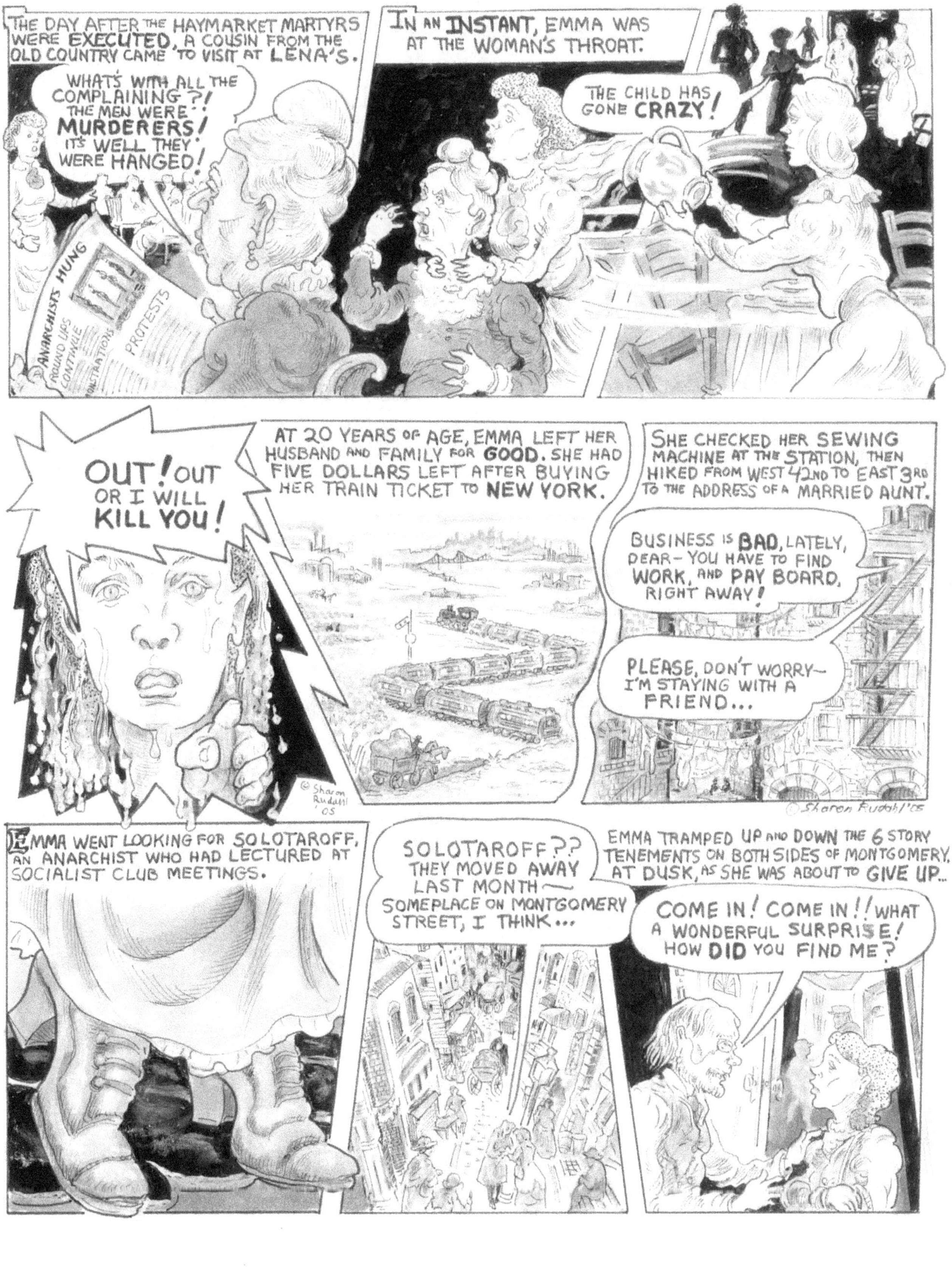

OUT! OUT OR I WILL KILL YOU!

© Sharon Rudahl '05

AT 20 YEARS OF AGE, EMMA LEFT HER HUSBAND AND FAMILY FOR GOOD. SHE HAD FIVE DOLLARS LEFT AFTER BUYING HER TRAIN TICKET TO NEW YORK.

SHE CHECKED HER SEWING MACHINE AT THE STATION, THEN HIKED FROM WEST 42ND TO EAST 3RD TO THE ADDRESS OF A MARRIED AUNT.

BUSINESS IS BAD, LATELY, DEAR– YOU HAVE TO FIND WORK, AND PAY BOARD, RIGHT AWAY!

PLEASE, DON'T WORRY– I'M STAYING WITH A FRIEND...

© Sharon Rudahl '05

EMMA WENT LOOKING FOR SOLOTAROFF, AN ANARCHIST WHO HAD LECTURED AT SOCIALIST CLUB MEETINGS.

SOLOTAROFF?? THEY MOVED AWAY LAST MONTH— SOMEPLACE ON MONTGOMERY STREET, I THINK...

EMMA TRAMPED UP AND DOWN THE 6 STORY TENEMENTS ON BOTH SIDES OF MONTGOMERY. AT DUSK, AS SHE WAS ABOUT TO GIVE UP...

COME IN! COME IN!! WHAT A WONDERFUL SURPRISE! HOW DID YOU FIND ME?

TAKE MY ROOM, TONITE~ I CAN STAY WITH A CLASSMATE...
TEA, MAYBE, AND A BISSEL CAKE?
SOLOTAROFF TOOK EMMA TO MEET THE MINKIN SISTERS—TWO RUSSIAN JEWISH WORKING GIRLS WHOSE FAMILY HAD A SPARE BED.
THANKS FOR BEING PATIENT ABOUT THE RENT...
AND HE TREATED THE 3 GIRLS TO DINNER AT SACH'S CAFE~ HEADQUARTERS FOR ALL THE EAST-SIDE BOHEMIANS AND RADICALS
SACH'S
THERE WERE THE MARXISTS, WHO BELIEVED INDUSTRIAL WORKERS WOULD LEAD INEVITABLE REVOLUTION,
THE HISTORY OF SOCIETY IS CLASS STRUGGLE!
FROM EACH ACCORDING TO HIS ABILITY, TO EACH ACCORDING TO HIS NEED!!
TOOT
THE DISICIPLES OF ANARCHIST M. BAKUNIN, WHO EXALTED ABSOLUTE INDIVIDUALISM,
THE PASSION FOR DESTRUCTION IS ALSO A CREATIVE PASSION!
WHACK
AND FOLLOWERS OF GENTLE COMMUNIST-ANARCHIST PETER KROPOTKIN...
COOPERATION IS NATURAL!!
A FEELING OF SOLIDARITY WILL GUIDE MEN'S ACTIONS...
ONE VOICE BOOMED ABOVE THE REST
EXTRA LARGE STEAK!! EXTRA CUP OF COFFEE! TWO SLICES OF PIE!
WHO IS THAT GLUTTON?
THAT'S ALEXANDER BERKMAN. HE CAN EAT FOR THREE. BUT HE RARELY HAS ENOUGH MONEY!
SHE DIFFUSES AN ATMOSPHERE OF STRENGTH AND VITALITY...
NO MORE THAN A BOY-BUT FIRST AND FOREMOST A DETERMINED REVOLUTIONIST!

ALEXANDER BERKMAN~
TWO YEARS YOUNGER THAN EMMA, BERKMAN CAME FROM SIMILAR, IF SLIGHTLY MORE REFINED, RUSSIAN JEWISH ROOTS. HIS FIRST REBELLION WAS DEFENDING A SERVANT GIRL AGAINST HIS HAUGHTY MOTHER. HE WAS EXPELLED FROM GYMNASIUM FOR WRITING "THERE IS NO GOD."
HERE GOES MY LAST WAGES!~ I HAD A FIGHT WITH THE FOREMAN AT THE CIGAR FACTORY.
I'M STARTING AS A PRINTER AT DIE FREIHEIT TOMORROW~ COME ALONG & I'LL INTRODUCE YOU TO JOHANN MOST!!
OH, YES, PLEASE!
©Sharon Rudahl '05
... SO I LEFT MY HUSBAND AND FAMILY... NOW I WANT TO LIVE LIKE VERA, IN 'WHAT IS TO BE DONE'
THAT WAS MY FAVORITE BOOK, TOO!!
TO ME, THE NIHILISTS WERE HEROES AND MARTYRS!
COULD ANYTHING BE NOBLER THAN TO DIE FOR A SUBLIME CAUSE?
DIE FREIHEIT
AND HERE IS OUR CURRENT HERO, JOHANN MOST...
ASK THEM TO WRITE A LINE-NOT THEY! TOO LAZY AND STUPID!!
MAY I PRESENT A NEW COMRADE~ MISS EMMA GOLDMAN...
WHERE DID YOU GET THAT SILKY BLOND HAIR?!
MY DEAR... THE PATH OF ANARCHISM IS HARD AND PAINFUL...
JOHANN MOST~ MORE THAN TWICE EMMA'S AGE. ORATOR, THEORIST, PUBLISHER, CELEBRITY. ONCE A MEMBER OF THE GERMAN REICHSTAG, HE HAD JUST BEEN RELEASED FROM PRISON IN EUROPE. MOST HID HIS DEFORMED JAW BEHIND A THICK BEARD...

JOHANN MOST TOOK EMMA UNDER HIS WING: ASSIGNING READING LISTS, ESCORTING HER TO THE OPERA, CONCERTS AND POSH RESTAURANTS...
MOST BECAME MY IDOL... I WORSHIPPED HIM...
ALL OVER THE WORLD, YOU ARE LOVED AND IDOLIZED...
ONE CAN BE VERY LONELY AMONG MILLIONS...
EMMA SHARED HER HOPES AND DREAMS WITH HIM...
YOU HAVE A READY TONGUE, MEIN KIND... I COULD TEACH YOU TO BE A GREAT SPEAKER, TO TAKE MY PLACE, WHEN I AM GONE...
TO YOUR FIRST PUBLIC SPEECH!!
CLINK
© Sharon Rudahl '05
COMRADE BERKMAN CONSIDERED JEALOUSY BOURGEOIS, BUT HE WAS ANNOYED...
MOST HAS NO RIGHT TO SQUANDER MONEY CONTRIBUTED TO THE MOVEMENT!!
TO EMMA FROM JOHANN
EMMA GAVE HER FIRST SHORT TALKS INVITING IMMIGRANT UNIONS TO THE ANNIVERSARY OF HAYMARKET.
A GRAND COMMEMORATION, AT THE COOPER UNION...

For the Haymarket Anniversary, Emma, Berkman, his cousin Fedya, and the Minkin Sisters contributed a huge laurel wreath.
I'll lift you up, little comrade!
Haymar Never For et
Local
Johann Most's speech that night was especially eloquent and fiery.
A wild, passionate cry against the terrible thing that had happened in Chicago...
As he walked Emma home, Berkman recounted the story of the nihilist lovers who assassinated the Czar...
Sophia had every chance to escape, but she refused...
She would share the fate of her comrade.
If I ever love again, I will give myself without being bound by the rabbi or the law!!
My girl, my brave sailor girl...
Sasha...
My Sasha...

The Strongest Link
Emma, Sasha, his cousin Fedya, and Helen Minkin established an anarchist commune in a coldwater flat on 42nd Street.
From the first, we agreed to share everything...
Their lives were crammed with meetings and protests
Helen toiled at a corset factory...
Emma sewed piecework at the flat, and did most of the housework...
Sasha went back to his old job, rolling cigars...
Fedya was an artist. He sometimes sold a portrait or landscape, but most of his money went for paints and canvas.
Could one love two people at the same time?!
Pickles
Fedya drew me to him by his sensitive response and his love of beauty...
Sasha Berkman did not believe in possessiveness. But he was annoyed.
Fedya is a mother's darling who even accepts money from home...
If I let him, he'd spend all his money on useless things!
SOLD
To Emma from Fedya
To Emma from Fedya
SOLD
©Sharon Rudahl 05

JOHANN MOST PLOTTED TO GET HER AWAY FROM BOTH SASHA AND FEDYA...
CLEVELAND
ROCHESTER
BUFFALO
YOUR FIRST SERIOUS SPEAKING TOUR!!
I HAVE CHOSEN THE SUBJECT, AND I WILL HELP YOU PREPARE!
AS MOST'S DISCIPLE, EMMA WAS SENT TO PERSUADE WORKERS NOT TO FOCUS ON WINNING THE 8 HOUR DAY.
OUR COMRADES IN CHICAGO LOST THEIR LIVES FOR THAT CAUSE!
BUT THESE PETTY FIGHTS DISTRACT FROM THE BATTLE AGAINST CAPITALISM!
EMMA HAD 3 WEEKS TO GET READY.
DON'T WORRY ABOUT THE CLEANING AND COOKING! WE'RE PROUD TO HELP YOU...
YOU MUST THINK ONLY OF HOW USEFUL YOU WILL BECOME TO THE CAUSE...
GOD AND THE STATE
BE BOLD! BE ARROGANT! IF YOU CAN MAKE PEOPLE LAUGH, SAILING WILL BE EASY...
3
2
© Sharon Rudahl 05
IN ROCHESTER, EMMA DID NOT CONTACT HER ESTRANGED FAMILY. BUT HELENA SAW A FLYER PROMOTING THE NEW SPEAKER, AND SECRETLY CAME TO SEE HER BABY SISTER.
IF OUR PARENTS KNEW WHAT YOU WERE UP TO, THEY WOULD NEVER GET OVER THE SHOCK!
FACING A REAL AUDIENCE FOR THE FIRST TIME, EMMA WENT NUMB. SHE REPEATED HER LESSONS BY ROTE...
AS JOHANN MOST SAYS... BLAH, BLAH, BLAH... IRON LAW OF WAGES... BLAH... FIGHT CAPITALISM...
DIE FREI
ARBEITE

IN CLEVELAND, EMMA GOT BY WITH "CHEAP JOKES AND BITTER THRUSTS." NO ONE EXPECTED MUCH FROM AN UNKNOWN YOUNG WOMAN.
WHY BLAME THE CAPITALISTS, WHEN YOU WORKERS WOULD TRADE YOUR FUTURE FOR A COUPLE HOURS AT THE BEER HALL?!
HOW DID A NICE GIRL LIKE YOU BECOME AN ANARCHIST?
IN CHICAGO, AN OLD WORKER ACCOSTED HER
TONITE: AGAINST THE 8 HOUR DAY MISS EMMA GOLDMA courtesy of DIE FREI
I UNDERSTAND YOU YOUNG FOLKS ARE IMPATIENT WITH SMALL DEMANDS...
...BUT I WON'T LIVE TO SEE THE REVOLUTION!
WILL I NEVER HAVE A LITTLE TIME FOR READING, OR TO WALK OUT IN THE OPEN AIR?
WHEN EMMA ROSE TO SPEAK THAT NIGHT, SHE THOUGHT OF HER YOUTH SPENT IN BITTER DRUDGERY, THE MANY LIVES CRUSHED TO ENRICH THE POWERFUL... SHE FORGOT MOST'S SCRIPT, AND POURED OUT HER OWN VISION.
"THE AUDIENCE VANISHED, THE HALL DISAPPEARED. I WAS CONSCIOUS ONLY OF MY OWN ECSTATIC SONG..."
© Sharon Rudahl 05
EMMA HAD FOUND HER ART- ONE LOST IN OUR AGE OF ELECTRONIC MEDIA. SHE WAS ONE OF THE GREAT ORATORS. PEOPLE FLOCKED TO HEAR THEM LIKE FAMOUS SINGERS OR MUSICAL VIRTUOSI, EXPECTING TO BE TRANSPORTED AND RENEWED...
I HAVE A DREAM...
I MISSED YOU SO, EMMA, I WON'T SEND YOU ON TOUR AGAIN!
I'M NOT TAKING ORDERS FROM YOU ANYMORE, JOHANN...
VIPER! SNAKE!! HEARTLESS COQUETTE!

VIOLETS AT THE HEIGHT OF WINTER, WITH THOUSANDS OUT OF WORK AND HUNGRY!!
MOST BEGGED ME TO MARRY HIM AND BE THE MOTHER OF HIS CHILDREN. OF COURSE, I REFUSED...
I DO LOVE YOU, EMMA... BUT THE TRUE REVOLUTIONARY MUST BE WILLING TO GIVE UP EVERYTHING.
SOMEDAY I WILL SHOW YOU HOW GREAT MY DEVOTION CAN BE...
© Sharon Rudahl '05
IN 1890, WHEN EMMA WAS 21, SHE HELPED ORGANIZE A STRIKE OF CLOAKMAKERS, IMMIGRANT WOMEN WHO WORKED 14 HOURS A DAY, FOR $9 A WEEK. AS AN ANARCHIST, SHE WAS SKEPTICAL OF ALL ORGANIZATIONS, INCLUDING UNIONS... BUT AFTER MEETING THE OLD WORKER IN CHICAGO, EMMA NEVER AGAIN LET DOCTRINE STAND IN THE WAY OF A GOOD FIGHT.
CONCERTS AND DANCES WERE HELD TO ATTRACT WORKING GIRLS AND ENCOURAGE THEM TO JOIN THE STRIKE.
COMRADE, IT'S UNDIGNIFIED FOR AN ORGANIZER TO DANCE~ ESPECIALLY SO WILDLY!
MIND YOUR OWN BUSINESS!
I DO NOT BELIEVE OUR BEAUTIFUL CAUSE SHOULD DENY LIFE AND JOY!!
EVERYONE HAS A RIGHT TO FREEDOM AND SELF-EXPRESSION, THE RIGHT TO ENJOY BEAUTIFUL, RADIANT THINGS!
TWO YEARS BEFORE, THE 1ST INTERNATIONAL CONGRESS IN PARIS HAD DECLARED MAY 1 A HOLIDAY OF LABOR. THE CALL WENT OUT FOR MASS MEETINGS, PARADES AND STRIKES. EMMA WAS CHOSEN TO BE THE ANARCHIST SPEAKER AT N.Y.'S UNION SQUARE.
THE SOCIALISTS REFUSE TO LET US PUT UP OUR STAGE!
THEN I'LL SPEAK FROM THE BACK OF THIS WAGON!!

THE DRIVER CRACKED HIS WHIP, THE HORSE TROTTED OFF. AS EMMA SPOKE, THE CROWD FOLLOWED HER OUT OF UNION SQUARE, TEN BLOCKS BEFORE THE POLICE CHASED THEM AWAY.
EXPRESS
NEW YORK DAILY
GIRL RABBLE-ROUSER WAVING RED FLAG LEADS ANGRY MOB!
EXTRA!! READ ALL ABOUT IT!
BESIDES AGITATING AND KEEPING HOUSE, EMMA HAD BEEN SEWING PIECEWORK, UP TO 16 HOURS A DAY. SHE BECAME WEAK, AND SUFFERED MYSTERIOUS PAINS...
IT'S FEMALE TROUBLE. IF SHE DOESN'T HAVE AN OPERATION, THE CRAMPS WILL RECUR, AND SHE WILL NEVER BEAR CHILDREN.
IN THAT ERA, SURGERY WAS DANGEROUS AND UNCERTAIN. MANY IMMIGRANTS THOUGHT OF HOSPITALS AS DEATH TRAPS. EMMA MAY HAVE FEARED DISABILITY OR THE EXPENSE OF CONVALESCENCE. SHE NEVER ATTEMPTED TO CORRECT HER INFERTILITY.
TO FULFILL MY MISSION, I MUST REMAIN UNHAMPERED AND UNTIED...
FEDYA HAD GONE TO WORK FOR A PHOTOGRAPHER IN SPRINGFIELD, MASS. HE OFFERED EMMA AN UNDEMANDING JOB TAKING ORDERS. SASHA JOINED THEM, AND THE COMRADES SET UP THEIR OWN PHOTO STUDIO...
NEW YORK PHOTO
THAT'S THE LAST OF OUR SAVINGS, GONE FOR RENT— AND FEWER ORDERS THAN LAST MONTH!
THEN LET'S HIRE A BUGGY, AND GO LOOK FOR NEW CUSTOMERS!
© Sharon Rudahl '06
THEY SCOURED THE NEW ENGLAND COUNTRYSIDE, TO DRUM UP ORDERS FOR FAMILY PHOTOS AND HAND-TINTED MEMORIAL PORTRAITS... THE NATIVES WERE UNIMPRESSED.
PHOTOS
WHOA!
THE AMERICAN FARMER IS REALLY A SMALL CAPITALIST!!
THE WAY THE LITTLE LADY COOKS, YOU FOLKS SHOULD OPEN A LUNCHROOM INSTEAD.

SASHA HAMMERED AND SAWED, FEDYA PAINTED AND DECORATED. EMMA BREWED COFFEE AND STUFFED CABBAGE ROLLS...
NEW YORK DINE
IN 6 MONTHS, THEY PAID OFF THE LOAN FROM THEIR LANDLORD, AND WERE ABLE TO INVEST IN A SODA-WATER FOUNTAIN...
"LATEST DEVELOPMENTS IN HOMESTEAD ~ FAMILIES OF STRIKERS EVICTED FROM COMPANY HOUSING..."
OH NO!
HOMESTEAD
EVICTIONS
WHEN MANAGER HENRY CLAY FRICK CUT WAGES, THERE WAS A BITTER STRIKE AT THE CARNEGIE-OWNED STEEL PLANT IN HOMESTEAD, PENNSYLVANIA...
ARE YOU OKAY, YOUNG LADY??
STRIKE
ARRESTS
HOMESTE
EVICTI
THE COFFEE AND ICE CREAM ARE FREE, MISTER— BUT PLEASE GIVE ME YOUR NEWSPAPER!
AT MIDNIGHT OF JUNE 6, 1892, 300 PINKERTON GOONS WERE TOWED UPRIVER. ARMED WORKERS MET THEM AT HOMESTEAD.
I MUST ASK YOU TO LEAVE— I'M CLOSING THE STORE...
IT SOUNDS LIKE THE AWAKENING OF THE AMERICAN WORKER!!
HOMESTEAD
BATTLE
THE GREAT MOMENT HAS COME AT LAST!
AFTER A SEVEN HOUR GUN-BATTLE, 7 PINKERTONS AND 9 WORKERS WERE DEAD, SCORES BADLY WOUNDED.
THE LUNCHROOM IS YOURS! WE HAVE TO GO... HELP A SICK FRIEND!!
HERE ARE THE KEYS...
YOU'RE CRAZY- YOU'D MAKE A BUNDLE SELLING ICE CREAM THIS SUMMER!
WORKING ONE LAST NIGHT AT THE DINER, THE COMRADES CLEARED $75.00, AND RETURNED TO NEW YORK. THE THREE PLANNED AN ATTENTAT ~ AN ACT OF PROPAGANDA BY DEED ~ INTENDED TO AROUSE THE MASSES.
THE TIME FOR MANIFESTOS IS PAST... FRICK MUST BE MADE TO STAND THE CONSEQUENCES!!
WE WILL GO TO HOMESTEAD WITH YOU!

WORKING SECRETLY AT NIGHT IN THE BASEMENT OF THEIR NEW YORK FLAT, SASHA RESEARCHED RECIPES FOR A DYNAMITE BOMB
SCIENCE of REVOLUTIONARY WARFARE BY JOHANN MOST
DANGER
© Sharon Rudahl 2006
WHILE HE EXPERIMENTED, EMMA KEPT WATCH...

A WEEK'S WORK AND FORTY PRECIOUS DOLLARS WASTED ~ THE BOMB FAILED TO EXPLODE!!
DANGER
FFzzzzzzzTTTTTTTT
MAYBE MOST'S DIRECTIONS ARE WRONG!
THE CELLAR IS DAMP ~ BABKAH DOESN'T RISE IF THE BAKING SODA IS DAMP...
EMMA WENT FROM COMRADE TO COMRADE, TRYING TO BORROW MONEY OR WEAPONS...
DIE FREIHEIT
AN ACT ON THE LIFE OF FRICK? OF COURSE, I WOULD HAVE TO FIRST CONSULT WITH OUR PEOPLE IN EUROPE...
FEH!!
SASHA, FEDYA, & EMMA HAD $15.00 LEFT ~ ENOUGH FOR ONLY ONE PERSON'S TRAIN TICKET, AND A FEW NIGHTS AT A CHEAP HOTEL...
LET ME GO ALONE...
YOU'LL NEED AT LEAST $10.00 TO BUY A GUN
ANOTHER $10 FOR DECENT CLOTHES, TO GET INTO FRICK'S OFFICE...
RECALLING THE NOBLE PROSTITUTE SONYA, OF DOSTOYEVSKY'S CRIME AND PUNISHMENT, EMMA WIRED HELENA FOR A FEW DOLLARS ~ JUST ENOUGH TO BUY FRINGE & FEATHERS!
SURELY, I CAN ATTRACT SOME GENEROUS GENTLEMAN ON 42ND STREET...
SASHA IS GIVING HIS LIFE AND YOU SHRINK AT GIVING YOUR BODY, MISERABLE COWARD
EMMA TRAMPED BACK AND FORTH NERVOUSLY UNTIL ALMOST MIDNIGHT
HOW ABOUT A DRINK, LITTLE GIRL?

SHE LED HIM THRU THE BACK ENTRANCE OF A SALOON ON 13TH STREET...
YOU'RE A NOVICE AT THE TRADE, AREN'T YOU?
HOW DID YOU KNOW?
THERE'S NOTHING IN PROSTITUTION, UNLESS YOU HAVE THE KNACK FOR IT.
BUT THOUSANDS OF GIRLS ARE DRIVEN TO SELL THEMSELVES BY ECONOMIC NECESSITY!
YOU HAVEN'T GOT THE KNACK, THAT'S ALL THERE IS TO IT!!
HERE'S $25.00 FOR YOUR TROUBLE... GO GET OUT OF THOSE CHEAP SHOES!
© Sharon Rudahl '06
AT LEAST LET ME WRITE YOU AN I.O.U.!
YOU'RE AN AWFULLY NICE KID...
DON'T WORRY~ I'M 61, AND I'VE OFTEN DONE FOOLISH THINGS...
WITH EMMA'S $25.00, SASHA BOUGHT A DAGGER AND A GUN
HE ALSO PROVIDED HIMSELF WITH A NITROGLYCERIN SUICIDE CAPSULE.
ON JULY 22, 1892, BERKMAN FORCED HIS WAY INTO HENRY CLAY FRICK'S PRIVATE OFFICE AND FIRED THREE SHOTS...
BANG! BANG! BANG!
CARPENTERS WORKING IN THE BUILDING RUSHED IN, AND KNOCKED SASHA BERKMAN TO THE GROUND WITH A HAMMER.
BUT SASHA MANAGED TO CRAWL OVER AND STAB FRICK IN THE THIGH.

AT THE STATION HOUSE, POLICE NEARLY BROKE SASHA'S JAW, PRYING LOOSE THE NITRO SUICIDE CAPSULE.
WHAT'S THIS, THEN??
CANDY...
"ASSASSIN OVER-POWERED AFTER DESPERATE STRUGGLE..."
"FRICK LIVES BUT HIS WOUNDS ARE FATAL"
"FRICK MAKING STEADY RECOVERY"...
"THE PUBLIC DEMANDS POLICE ROUND UP THE INSTIGATORS~ JOHANN MOST, EMMA GOLDMAN, AND THEIR ILK"...
JULY 23 TUESDAY
AUGUST
SEPT 1 MONDAY
THEIR FLAT WAS RANSACKED BY DETECTIVES. EMMA WENT INTO HIDING WITH HER GRANDMOTHER, THE KÖNIGSBERG SMUGGLER, NOW RUNNING A GROCERY ON AVE. B...
FAIR-WEATHER REVOLUTIONARIES RAN FOR COVER. JOHANN MOST EVEN ACCUSED SASHA OF BEING IN LEAGUE WITH THE BOSSES.
WHAT DID HE USE, THIS SLAYER OF TYRANTS — A TOY PISTOL??! NOW FRICK HAS PUBLIC SYMPATHY AND THE POLICE CAN ARREST US ALL!
© Sharon Rudahl
EMMA CAME TO THE MEETING EQUIPPED WITH A HORSE WHIP, CONCEALED UNDER HER LONG CLOAK...
I DEMAND PROOF OF YOUR INSINUATIONS AGAINST ALEXANDER BERKMAN!!
TRAITOR! COWARD!!
CRACK
FEDYA AND OTHER LOYAL FRIENDS HURRIED EMMA FROM THE HALL...
GET OUT BEFORE WE THROW YOU OUT!!
SHE COULD USE A GOOD BEATING!!

HENRY CLAY FRICK RECOVERED COMPLETELY. THE HOMESTEAD STRIKE WAS BROKEN. SASHA SPOKE IN HIS OWN DEFENSE AND GOT 22 YEARS INSTEAD OF THE EXPECTED 7 FOR ATTEMPTED MANSLAUGHTER. ALMOST FORTY YEARS WOULD PASS BEFORE EMMA, IN HER AUTOBIOGRAPHY, ADMITTED COMPLICITY IN THE PLOT.

"SASHA'S ACT, FOR WHICH HE ALONE WOULD PAY THE PRICE, WOULD REMAIN THE STRONGEST LINK IN THE CHAIN THAT BOUND ME TO HIM..."

THROUGHOUT HER LONG LIFE, HER MANY COMRADES AND LOVERS, TRAVELS AND ADVENTURES, EMMA WAS DEVOTED TO THIS ONE MAN.

©Sharon Rudahl '06

BLACKWELL'S ISLAND
©Sharon Rudahl '06
IN THE MONTHS AFTER THE HOMESTEAD ASSASSINATION ATTEMPT, EMMA WAS SHUNNED BY FORMER COMRADES. HER LANDLORD TURNED HER OUT. ANYONE WHO GAVE HER LODGING WAS TERRORIZED BY THE POLICE...
SOME NIGHTS SHE SAT IN A CAFE UNTIL DAWN...
Cafe
ROOM TO LET
OR RODE BACK AND FORTH TO THE BRONX IN A STREETCAR...
THE POOR OLD HORSES SEEMED AS TIRED AS ME...
EMMA FINALLY FOUND REFUGE IN A HOUSE OCCUPIED BY PROSTITUTES...

THE GIRLS WERE FRIENDLY, EAGER CUSTOMERS FOR EMMA'S SKILLED DRESS-MAKING...
LOVELY...
DO ME ONE IN PINK!!
WITH SOLOTAROFF, HER FIRST FRIEND IN NEW YORK, EMMA ORGANIZED SUPPORT FOR SASHA, WORKING TO COMMUTE HIS SENTENCE. WHEN ANARCHIST GROUPS IN THE MIDWEST INVITED HER TO SPEAK, EMMA, POSED AS SASHA'S MARRIED SISTER TO TRY TO VISIT HIM AT THE WESTERN FEDERAL PENITENTIARY.
WAIT HERE, WHILE I CONTACT THE WARDEN—
MRS. E. NIEDERMAN, SISTER OF PRISONER A-7— I'VE COME ALL THE WAY FROM RUSSIA TO SEE MY BROTHER!!
© Sharon Rudahl '06
БАЛОВЕНЬ!
МОЯ ВЛЮБЛЕН-НОСТЪ!
TALK ENGLISH! NO FOREIGN LANGUAGES HERE!!
I CLUTCH DESPERATELY AT THE THREAD THAT STILL BINDS ME TO THE LIVING— IT SEEMS TO UNRAVEL IN MY HANDS...
BUT THE SONIA THREAD I KNOW WILL REMAIN STRONG...
THE ATTENTAT FAILED, HER LOVER ENTOMBED, EMMA BEGAN TO DOUBT IF NOBLE ENDS JUSTIFY ANY MEANS... SEWING LONG DAYS AND ATTENDING MEETINGS EVERY NIGHT, SHE BECAME WEAK AND THIN...
IT'S TUBERCULOSIS, YOUNG LADY— YOU'LL DIE WITHOUT REST AND BETTER AIR!!

SISTER HELENA TOOK CHARGE~RENTING A ROOM NEXT TO A SUNNY GARDEN, NEAR HER OWN HOME IN ROCHESTER...
"SHE NURSED ME WITH UNFAILING LOVE AND CARE..."
BUT NOT EVEN T.B. COULD KEEP EMMA ON THE SIDELINES FOR LONG... IN 1893 A STOCK MARKET PANIC PLUMMETED INTO SEVERE DEPRESSION.
DAILY LEDGER
JOBLESS WORKERS STARVE
IMMIGRANT FAMILIES EVICTED
TEXTILE MILL SHUTS DOWN
FACTORIES CLOSE
RICH GET RICHER
STILL FAR FROM WELL, EMMA RUSHED BACK TO NEW YORK TO SET UP SOUP KITCHENS AND ORGANIZE HUNGER DEMONSTRATIONS.
ASK FOR WORK! IF THEY DO NOT GIVE YOU WORK, ASK FOR BREAD!!
IF THEY DO NOT GIVE YOU WORK OR BREAD...
TAKE THE BREAD!!!
RELIEF
GROT
THE NEXT DAY, EMMA WENT TO PHILADELPHIA, SCHEDULED TO ADDRESS A MASS MEETING OF THE UNEMPLOYED... SHE WAS MET BY DETECTIVES
YOU'RE UNDER ARREST!
EMMA!! EMMA!!
EMMA!! EMMA!!
THE CROWD MARCHED FROM UNION SQUARE UP 5TH AVENUE, SMASHING WINDOWS AND GRABBING LOAVES FROM BAKERS' SHELVES.
© Sharon Rudahl

SHE WAS ESCORTED TO CITY HALL, PENDING EXTRADITION TO NEW YORK...
NO NEED FOR HANDCUFFS, BOYS — I WON'T TRY TO RUN AWAY!!
WHEN EMMA WAS MARCHED OFF, THE OTHER GREAT U.S. WOMAN ANARCHIST STEPPED UP TO TAKE HER PLACE.
IT IS TO MEN AND WOMEN OF FEELING I SPEAK... WHOSE HEARTS SWELL WITH PITY AT THE TOIL OF WOMEN, THE WEARINESS OF CHILDREN, THE HELPLESSNESS OF STRONG MEN...
VOLTAIRINE DE CLEYRE 1866~1912
BORN INTO RURAL POVERTY IN MICHIGAN, EDUCATED AT A CONVENT, SHE SCORNED THE AUTHORITY OF CHURCH AND GOVERNMENT...
LET EVERY WOMAN ASK HERSELF: WHY AM I THE SLAVE OF MAN?
VOLTAIRINE BELIEVED ANARCHISM FLOWED NATURALLY FROM AMERICAN INDIVIDUALISM AND LOVE OF FREEDOM. IN HER SHORT, ILLNESS-PLAGUED LIFE, SHE WAS A FEARLESS AGITATOR, A PROLIFIC AND ELEGANT WRITER...
© Sharon Rudahl '06
EMMA AND VOLTAIRINE SHARED CORE BELIEFS. BUT THE TWO WOMEN WERE NEVER FRIENDS.
LOUD! FLAMBOYANT AND SELF-INDULGENT! SLOPPY AND DUMPY!!
PRIM AND CHARMLESS!! COLD AND STIFF AS A BOARD!
EMMA TURNED DOWN AN OFFER OF RELEASE IN EXCHANGE FOR SPYING ON OTHER RADICALS. SHE WAS SENTENCED TO ONE YEAR IN THE BLACKWELL ISLAND PENITENTIARY, FOR "INCITING TO RIOT"
AT FIRST, THE OTHER WOMEN PRISONERS AVOIDED EMMA...
WATCH OUT FOR THAT ONE — SHE'S A BLOOD-THIRSTY ANARCHIST!!
SHE DOESN'T BELIEVE IN OUR LORD JESUS!

BUT WHEN EMMA WAS PUT IN CHARGE OF THE PRISON SEWING SHOP, SHE SOON WON OVER THE WOMEN'S HEARTS...
IT'S YOUR JOB TO GET MORE WORK OUT OF THEM!
I REFUSE TO BE A SLAVEDRIVER!
ON SUNDAY AFTERNOONS, AFTER CHURCH SERVICES, THE INMATES HAD AN HOUR TO VISIT WITH EACH OTHER.
WE WORK IN THE PRISON LAUNDRY...
WE'D BE GLAD TO WASH YOUR SMOCK.
WHY DON'T YOU LET ME DARN THOSE STOCKINGS?
THE DAMP AND CHILL OF HER CELL GAVE EMMA A BAD ATTACK OF RHEUMATISM. IN THE PRISON HOSPITAL SHE WAS ATTENDED BY THE GENIAL DOCTOR WHITE...
"INCITING TO RIOT"?! PIFFLE! I DON'T BELIEVE YOU COULD HURT A FLY!!
DR. WHITE PUT EMMA TO WORK AS HIS NURSE, TEACHING HER TO TAKE PULSES, CHECK TEMPERATURES, AND PERFORM SIMPLE PROCEDURES.
"TUBERCULOSIS... PNEUMONIA... MISCARRIAGE.. PELLAGRA..."
© Sharon Rudahl '06
EMMA DENOUNCED THE HEAD MATRON FOR STEALING THE INVALIDS' SPECIAL RATIONS - SHE WAS LOCKED IN THE PUNISHMENT HOLE...
RELEASE THAT GIRL AT ONCE! I NEED HER ON THE WARD!!
FAMOUS CIVIL WAR-ERA ABOLITIONIST AND NEWSPAPER EDITOR JOHN SWINTON INSISTED ON VISITING EMMA.
FROM NOW ON, YOU'LL RECEIVE YOUR LETTERS AND PARCELS PROMPTLY!!
THE LADY SURE HAS A LOT OF ADMIRERS!

WITH FREQUENT REPORTS IN SWINTON'S NEWSPAPER, EMMA BECAME A JAILHOUSE CELEBRITY. FANS SENT BOXES OF BOOKS AND TOILETRIES. AUSTRIAN ANARCHISTS DELIVERED HOT MEALS FROM THEIR RESTAURANT. FEDYA HAD FRESH FRUIT ROWED OVER TO THE ISLAND TWICE A WEEK...
AND A BISSEL GEFILTE FISH FOR PESACH!
EMMA SHARED EVERYTHING WITH THE LESS FORTUNATE PRISONERS...
AMONG HER PILES OF MAIL WERE CODED PRISON LETTERS FROM SASHA BERKMAN.
"NOW YOU ARE INDEED MY SAILOR GIRL..."
BEFORE HER ARREST, EMMA GAVE SPEECHES IN RUSSIAN AND GERMAN. AT BLACKWELL'S ISLAND, SHE PERFECTED HER ENGLISH...
WALDEN BY HENRY DAVID THOREAU
NATURE RALPH WALDO EMERSON
SHE WAS TUTORED BY ONE REGULAR VISITOR— ED BRADY, A SCHOLARLY ANARCHIST FROM AUSTRIA, TEN YEARS HER SENIOR...
ED BRADY IMMIGRATED AFTER TEN YEARS IN PRISON FOR PUBLISHING ANARCHIST LITERATURE. HE AND EMMA MET AT THE FREE ALEXANDER BERKMAN SUPPORT MEETINGS.
I THOUGHT WE MIGHT WORK ON VOLTAIRE TODAY, DEAR...
ONLY IF YOU PROMISE TO READ MORE SHAKESPEARE ALOUD, AFTER...
IN SOLITARY CONFINEMENT, I ALWAYS READ ALOUD TO MYSELF— IT WAS THE ONLY WAY TO KEEP MY SANITY!
Les Lettres Philosophique Voltaire
© Sharon Rudahl '06

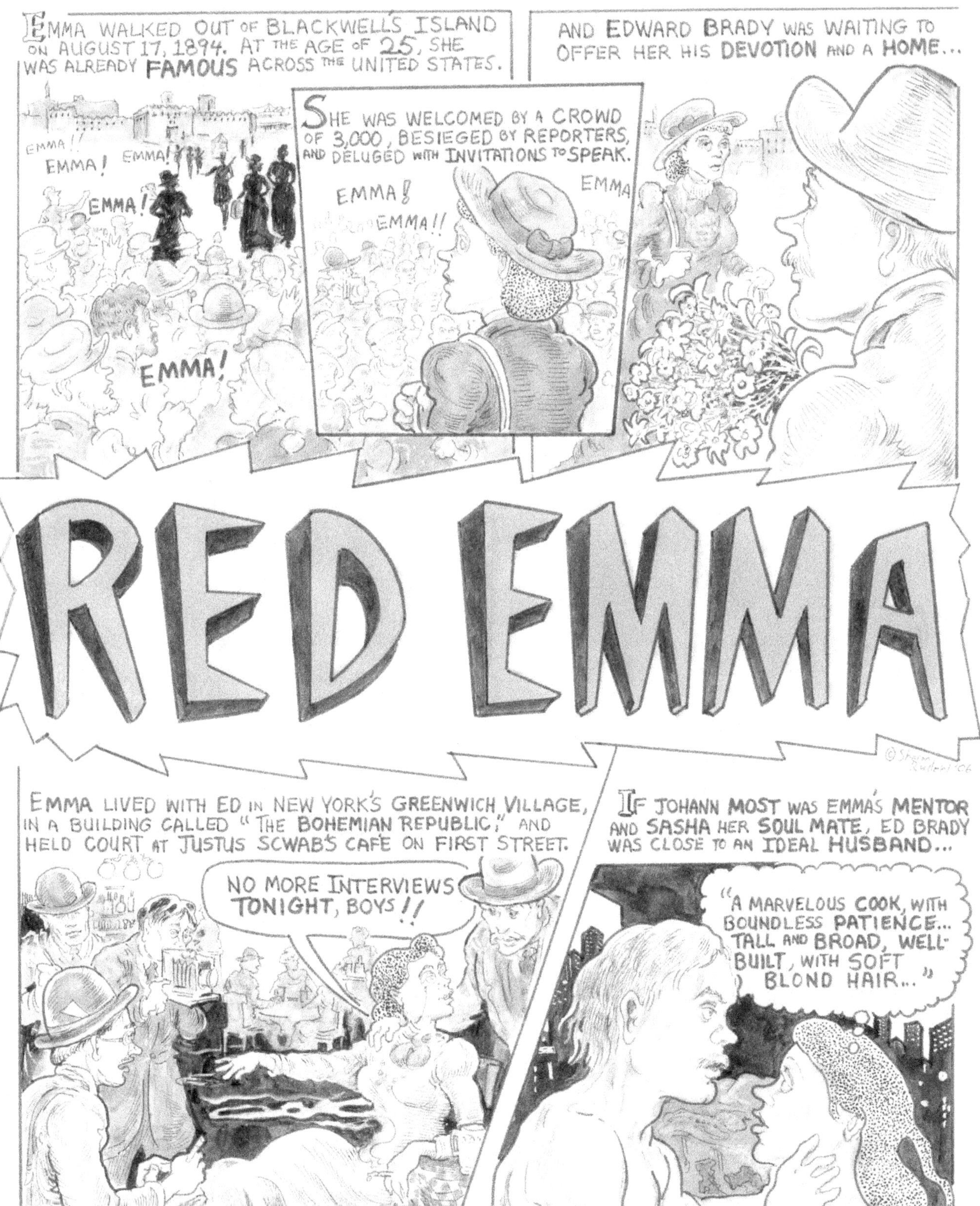

EMMA WALKED OUT OF BLACKWELL'S ISLAND ON AUGUST 17, 1894. AT THE AGE OF 25, SHE WAS ALREADY FAMOUS ACROSS THE UNITED STATES.
EMMA!!
EMMA! EMMA!
EMMA!
EMMA!
SHE WAS WELCOMED BY A CROWD OF 3,000, BESIEGED BY REPORTERS, AND DELUGED WITH INVITATIONS TO SPEAK.
EMMA!
EMMA!!
EMMA
AND EDWARD BRADY WAS WAITING TO OFFER HER HIS DEVOTION AND A HOME...
RED EMMA
EMMA LIVED WITH ED IN NEW YORK'S GREENWICH VILLAGE, IN A BUILDING CALLED "THE BOHEMIAN REPUBLIC," AND HELD COURT AT JUSTUS SCWAB'S CAFE ON FIRST STREET.
NO MORE INTERVIEWS TONIGHT, BOYS!!
IF JOHANN MOST WAS EMMA'S MENTOR AND SASHA HER SOUL MATE, ED BRADY WAS CLOSE TO AN IDEAL HUSBAND...
"A MARVELOUS COOK, WITH BOUNDLESS PATIENCE... TALL AND BROAD, WELL-BUILT, WITH SOFT BLOND HAIR..."

"WITH ED, I LEARNED FOR THE FIRST TIME THE MEANING OF THE GREAT LIFE-GIVING FORCE..."
AFTER HER STINT AT BLACKWELL'S ISLAND, EMMA WAS A STAR ON THE LECTURE CIRCUIT. VILIFIED AS DEMONIC RED EMMA BY THE PRESS, SHE MADE A POINT OF DRESSING SEDATELY IN BLACK. HER MEETINGS WERE SO OFTEN BROKEN UP BY THE POLICE, SHE ALWAYS CARRIED A BOOK TO READ, IN CASE OF ARREST*
* AUTHOR'S NOTE ~ IN MY DAY, THEY SEIZED ALL YOUR BOOKS AND PAPERS...
THOSE IN POWER NEVER LEARN, PERSECUTION IS THE LEAVEN OF REVOLUTION!
ARMY OF THE UNEMPLOYED
COXEY'S ARMY
SUPPORT PULLMAN STRIKE
PEOPLE WHO HEARD HER RECALL AN UNFORGETTABLY FIERCE AND PASSIONATE RABBLE-ROUSER... BUT SHE WAS ALSO WITTY AND QUICK ON HER FEET, ESPECIALLY CLEVER AT DEFLECTING HECKLERS.
BOO!
RED BITCH!
HISSSS!
GIT BACK TO YER KITCHEN!
BOOO!!
THE FULL DEVELOPMENT OF THE INDIVIDUAL IS ONLY POSSIBLE WHEN ONE HAS THE FREEDOM TO WORK AND THE FREEDOM TO CHOOSE THE CONDITIONS OF WORK!!
ARMY OF THE UNEMPLOYED
COXEY'S ARMY
PULLMAN STRIKE
SUPPOSING ONE OF YOU BOYS COMES UP HERE, AND SHOWS ME HOW TO KEEP THE REST QUIET?
DON'T YOU KNOW THE LAW GIVES ME THE RIGHT OF FREE SPEECH?!?
THE HELL IT DOES— I'M THE LAW!!
©Sharon Rudahl '06

ON THE ROAD, EMMA TOOK ORDERS FOR ED BRADY'S PHOTO ALBUMS, AS WELL AS MIXING IN LOCAL STRUGGLES AND CULTIVATING FRIENDSHIPS.
BEER
I BAPTIZE YOU IN THE NAME OF ANARCHY, JUSTICE, AND THE RIGHTS OF MAN!
INVITED TO ADDRESS A VETERANS' GROUP, EMMA ATTACKED PATRIOTISM...
HOME FOR DISABL VETERANS
LOVE FOR ONE'S COUNTRY IS EXPLOITED AS AN EXCUSE TO MAINTAIN HUGE ARMIES AT THE WORKING PEOPLE'S EXPENSE!
SHE MOCKED RELIGION IN FRONT OF CLERGYMEN...
THE MASSES HAVE LIVED IN HELL SO LONG, THEY WOULD NOT KNOW HOW TO BEHAVE IN HEAVEN!!
© Sharon Rudahl '06
AND RIDICULED THE BALLOT BEFORE WOMEN WHO PLACED ALL THEIR HOPES IN GAINING THE VOTE
WOMEN'S SUFFRAGE
VOTES FOR WOMEN
TO VOTE IN AN AMERICAN ELECTION IS TO INSULT YOUR OWN INTELLIGENCE!
EMMA REVELED IN OFF-THE-CUFF SPARRING.
DOES THE SPEAKER FAVOR KILLING OFF ALL RULERS?
THERE ARE SOME POTENTATES I WOULD KILL OFF BY ANY MEANS—THEY ARE IGNORANCE, SUPERSTITION, AND BIGOTRY!!!
HER BEST ATTENDED LECTURES WERE "THE NEW WOMAN" AND "FREE LOVE".
WHAT DOES LOVE HAVE TO DO WITH THAT POOR LITTLE CHURCH- AND STATE-BEGOTTEN WEED, MARRIAGE?!?

SOMETIMES A FAN GOT THE WRONG IDEA!!
HOTEL
?
BANG! BANG!
OPEN UP, YOU GORGEOUS WILD WOMAN!!!
GET LOST!
BUT I THOUGHT YOU BELIEVED IN FREE LOVE?!
THOUGH SHE WAS A STAR ORATOR, EMMA REFUSED TO RAISE TICKET PRICES, AND LET IN STUDENTS AND THE UNEMPLOYED FREE. TRAVEL EXPENSES ATE UP MUCH OF THE PROCEEDS. IN NEW YORK, SHE CARED FOR THE SICK, HER CHILDHOOD CAREER CHOICE~NURSING PRIVATE PATIENTS DIRECTED TO HER BY BLACKWELL'S DR. WHITE.
TOO MANY BABIES, TOO QUICKLY
I'M AFRAID IT'S A HOPELESS CASE, EMMA... SHE'S GOT NO FIGHT LEFT...
SINCE EMMA HAD NO OFFICIAL QUALIFICATIONS, HER ONLY CLIENTS WERE POOR IMMIGRANT WOMEN
MOMMA SAYS SHE CAN'T PAY YOU, WOULD YOU TAKE THESE PIEROGI, INSTEAD?
SHARE THEM WITH YOUR SISTERS, SHEINDELE...
EMMA SAW FOR HERSELF WHAT UNRELIEVED FERTILITY MEANT FOR WOMEN...
THIS ONE TRIED THROWING HERSELF DOWN THE STAIRS TO END HER PREGNANCY.

HOPING TO FIND SERVICES FOR HER PATIENTS' FAMILIES, EMMA VISITED THE SETTLEMENT ON HENRY ST.~ ONE OF THE COMMUNITY CENTERS RECENTLY FOUNDED BY JANE ADDAMS...
"TEACHING THE POOR TO EAT WITH A FORK IS ALL VERY WELL— BUT WHAT GOOD DOES IT DO IF THEY HAVE NO FOOD?"
OUR MISSION IS TO ELEVATE THE LOWER CLASS!
ED BRADY MISSED EMMA DREADFULLY WHEN SHE WAS ON SPEAKING TOURS, AND FELT ASHAMED THAT HER INCOME WAS NEEDED TO MAKE ENDS MEET.
IF I WERE A HOD-CARRIER OR A TAILOR I COULD SUPPORT A FAMILY... BUT I'M JUST A USELESS INTELLECTUAL!
REACTIONARY!
EMMA GOT RESTLESS WHEN SHE STAYED HOME TOO LONG...
PRACTICAL NURSES ARE PAID LIKE SERVANTS. I SHOULD TAKE A CERTIFIED TRAINING COURSE.
YOU NEED MONEY FOR ANYTHING, I LEND YOU!!
A PROSPEROUS COMRADE FROM HUNGARY HIRED ED TO MANAGE HIS CARPENTRY SHOP.
NOW I CAN SEND YOU TO NURSING SCHOOL IN VIENNA! THAT'S WHERE YOU'LL GET THE MOST SCIENTIFIC TRAINING...
IF SHE HAD A REAL CAREER, SHE'D GIVE UP TOURING!
IT WOULD BE EASIER TO PASS MY EXAMS IN GERMAN...
I CAN GIVE SPEECHES IN EUROPE!!
© Sharon Rudahl '06
JUST THINK, FEDYA, VIENNA! THEATRE, ART, IDEAS!!
BUT NOW I WORK FOR THE PLUTOCRATS, YOU MUST ALLOW ME TO PAY YOUR TRAVEL EXPENSES!
FEDYA HAD BECOME A POPULAR COMMERCIAL ILLUSTRATOR, ON HIS WAY TO A CAREER IN HOLLYWOOD.
ON AUGUST 15, 1895, TEN YEARS AFTER SHE ARRIVED PENNILESS IN NEW YORK, EMMA SAILED FOR ENGLAND..
SHE TRAVELED AS MRS. E.G. BRADY, BUT HER THOUGHTS WERE WITH SASHA, LANGUISHING IN THE PENITENTIARY.

In Victorian England, Emma was shocked by the appalling misery of the lower classes
Nothing compared in brutality and degradation with the sights I witnessed in London's East End...
Gin
The British government allows its subjects free speech, lest they rebel at their fearful destitution!!
Bloody rot!!!
Put a sock in it!
End is near
'Ear, 'ear!
Don't mind, dearie, it's a good old British custom!
Encouraged by British comrades, she gave speeches in Glasgow and Leeds, and dared the hecklers in Hyde Park...
Emma was welcomed by anarchist immortals Errico Malatesta of Italy, Louise Michel of the doomed Paris Commune and Russian Prince Peter Kropotkin ~ an exile in the placid London suburb of Bromley.
The average Englishman loves to think he is free, it helps him to forget his misery...
Krankenhaus
Please, try the strawberries ~ I grow them myself!
This table and chairs he made in his own workshop!
She was reluctant to leave England — but nursing school began October 1st.
Fin de siecle Vienna ~ more fascinating than Ed Brady's nostalgic stories...
Übermensch
Oriental Railway
Art Nouveau
Klimt
Mahler
Schnitzler
Leit Motif
Nietzsche
Duse
Psychoanalysis
Rothschilds
Socialists
Austro-Hungary
Hapsburgs
Waltz
Emma even attended a lecture by controversial Dr. Freud...
Id... Ego... Superego!!
For the first time I grasped the full significance of sexual repression!

EMMA'S TEACHERS WERE WORLDLY AND WELL-INFORMED. IN ONE YEAR, SHE EARNED CERTIFICATES IN NURSING AND MIDWIFERY.
YOU'LL SEE A LOT OF THIS DISEASE!
FEW CAN RESIST THE CHARM OF ITS ORIGIN, OR AFFORD THE PRICE OF IT'S CURE!
FEDYA SENT HER RETURN TICKET, PLUS $100.00 FOR CLOTHES...
EMMA BOUGHT 2 SUITCASES-FULL OF BOOKS INSTEAD
ED BRADY WAS MAKING GOOD MONEY AT THE CARPENTRY SHOP- $15.00 A WEEK. HE THREW A WELCOME HOME BANQUET FOR EMMA, AND RENTED A NEW FLAT.
NOW WE CAN LIVE LIKE A REAL HUSBAND AND WIFE!!
WITH HER CERTIFICATES, EMMA EXPECTED TO FIND WORK AS A PROFESSIONAL MIDWIFE.
I'M SORRY, EMMA... THE UPTOWN LADIES INSIST ON BEING ATTENDED BY MALE DOCTORS.
DR. WHITE REFERRED HER TO HIS CHARITY PATIENTS- PROSTITUTES, DRUG ADDICTS, POOR IMMIGRANTS. SHE WAS STILL PAID AND TREATED LIKE A SERVANT... OVER ED'S OBJECTIONS, EMMA WENT BACK TO THE LECTURE CIRCUIT...
STELLA!!
ON TOUR THROUGH ROCHESTER, SHE SAW HER FAMILY FOR THE FIRST TIME IN FIVE YEARS...
YOU'RE GROWING TO LOOK MORE LIKE YOUR TANTE HELENA... NOT SO BLONDE AS MOMMA LENA...
BUT IT'S TANTE EMMA, I LOVE BEST OF ALL!
I HATE THE PEOPLE WHO ARE MEAN TO YOU. WHEN I GROW UP, I WILL FIGHT FOR YOU!!
AFTER A LIFETIME OF OVERWORK AND HARASSMENT, EMMA'S FATHER ABRAHAM WAS A BROKEN SHADOW.
I BEGAN TO REGARD HIM AS ONE OF THE EXPLOITED AND OPPRESSED.
©Sharon Rudahl '06

HELENA HAD MADE AN UNROMANTIC LATE MARRIAGE TO JACOB HOCSTEIN. THEY RAN A SMALL STEAMSHIP AGENCY.
OUR PRODIGY, DAVID!
BROTHER HERMANN DISAPPOINTED THE FAMILY BY LEAVING SCHOOL TO WORK IN A MACHINE SHOP, BUT BABY BROTHER YEGOR LONGED FOR MORE...
I WANT TO GO BACK TO SCHOOL, TO STUDY MEDICINE!
YOU HAVE BECOME MY HEROINE...
YOU HAVE BEEN IN PRISON, YOU ARE IN TOUCH WITH THE PEOPLE, AND THE AIMS OF YOUTH!
© SHARON RUDAHL '06
EMMA'S STRONG-WILLED MOTHER TAUBE HAD COME INTO HER OWN - A POWERFUL ORGANIZER FOR JEWISH CHARITIES.
THIS PROVED TO BE MY FIRST UNCLOUDED VISIT WITH MY FAMILY...
LADIES! ENOUGH KVETCHING, ALREADY!!
DON'T THINK YOU CAN SHUT ME UP, REBBE! THE WHOLE U.S. GOVERNMENT CAN'T MAKE MY DAUGHTER EMMA SHUT UP!
EMMA'S TOUR CONTINUED ACROSS THE COUNTRY
WOOOOOOOOO
WOOOOOOO
CHUGGA CHUGGA
CHUGGA CHUGGA!!
CHUGGA CHUGGA
THE DENVER POST
GOLDMAN UNDER MANAGEMENT OF NEW MEXICO MILLIONAIRE
DETROIT STAR
FREE LOVER SPEAKS FROM PULPIT
San Francisco Examiner
SPANISH-AMERICAN WAR DECLARED!
RED EMMA OUTRAGES PATRIOTS
Philadelphia INQUIRER FINAL
EMMA GOLDMAN DRINKS LIKE A TROOPER
Pittsburg Leader
MISS GOLDMAN DOES NOT LOOK LIKE SHE CARRIES BOMBS IN HER POCKETS
Chicago Tribune FINAL
EMMA GOLDMAN LAYS WREATH AT HAYMARKET

HOME AT LAST!
I'LL JUST HAVE TIME FOR A WASH, BEFORE THE SUMMIT TEXTILE STRIKE MEETING... HOW HAVE YOU BEEN DOING, ED?
THIS MANIA FOR MEETINGS! I CAN'T STAND YOU ALWAYS PUTTING YOURSELF IN DANGER.
YOU WANT ME ONLY AS YOUR WIFE!
I TRY TO STIFLE MY LOVE, AND MEET YOU ON TERMS OF COMRADESHIP... BUT I CAN'T DO IT.
DURING THE YEAR EMMA STUDIED NURSING IN VIENNA, SASHA BERKMAN APPLIED TO THE BOARD OF PARDONS. ED BRADY AND VOLTAIRINE DE CLEYRE CAMPAIGNED FOR HIS RELEASE. SASHA BECAME CHEERFUL, ORGANIZING FROM BEHIND BARS, AND EVEN PUTTING OUT A PRISON NEWSLETTER...
BEFORE YOU RUSH OFF TO YOUR MEETING, EMMA, YOU'D BEST HAVE A LOOK AT THIS...
Board of Pardons
"THE BOARD REFUSES TO CONSIDER PARDON... A NEW APPLICATION MAY BE FILED AFTER THE PRISONER COMPLETES HIS FIRST TWELVE YEAR SENTENCE..."
WHY WON'T YOU BE BIG AND FREE, AND TAKE WHAT I CAN GIVE?!
©Sharon Rudahl 06
OH, ED! THAT PARDON WAS SASHA'S ONE HOPE!!
TERRIFIED THAT BERKMAN WOULD NEVER LEAVE THE WESTERN PENITENTIARY ALIVE, EMMA AGREED TO A DESPERATE ESCAPE PLAN.
"IT WILL NOT FAIL IF MY INSTRUCTIONS ARE FAITHFULLY CARRIED OUT..."

SASHA PLOTTED WITH TONY, A PRISON PAL DUE FOR RELEASE, ENTRUSTING HIM WITH DIAGRAMS AND MEASUREMENTS TO DIG A TUNNEL FROM OUTSIDE.
SASHA'S CELL
WATCHTOWER III
LATRINES
WATCHTOWER II
GUARD HOUSE II
WATCHTOWER I
BOARDEN STREET
STERLING STREET
WESTERN PENITENTIARY
ROOMING HOUSE
ALLEY
GUARD HOUSE I
N
E
W
S
EMMA SELECTED ERIK MORTEN, A STALWART NORWEGIAN COMRADE, TO SUPERVISE SASHA'S GETAWAY...
I CAN EASILY RAISE TONY'S MONEY... BUT CAN WE TRUST HIM?!?
DON'T WORRY! I'LL BE IN PITTSBURGH WHEN TONY'S SPRUNG, I CAN KEEP MY EYE ON HIM.
WE'LL HAVE TO WORK SLOWLY... CAN BERKMAN HOLD OUT?
AS LONG AS HE HAS HOPE!!
EMMA HAD TWO WEALTHY GERMAN-AMERICAN FANS WITH A TASTE FOR RADICAL POLITICS— CARL SCHMIDT AND HERMAN MILLER...
WHAT AN HONOR FOR US, TO ENTERTAIN THE FAMOUS EMMA GOLDMAN!!
FAMOUS?? MAYBE SO, GENTLEMEN... BUT MY LECTURES BARELY PAY EXPENSES!
ARTZ
...AND WORKING AS A PRACTICAL NURSE, I'M PAID ABOUT AS MUCH AS THE GIRLS IN THE MILLS!!!
BUT THAT'S A DISGRACE!
YOU SHOULD COMPLETE YOUR MEDICAL DEGREE, MISS EMMA!!
CARL AND I WOULD BE DELIGHTED TO SPONSOR YOUR STUDIES!
© Sharon Rudahl '06

© Sharon Rudahl '06
MY NURSING CERTIFICATES AREN'T RESPECTED HERE, ED. A MEDICAL DEGREE WOULD MEAN SECURITY...
BUT MORE IMPORTANT, IF I'M IN EUROPE WHEN SASHA BREAKS OUT- I CAN'T BE ARRESTED AS A SUSPECT!!
THIS TIME, I SWEAR, I WON'T BE WAITING FOR YOU EMMA...
IN NOVEMBER 1899, EMMA BOARDED A STEAMSHIP BACK TO EUROPE. SHE PLANNED TO OVERSEE SASHA'S ESCAPE, WHILE STUDYING TO COMPLETE HER MEDICAL DEGREE... MANY FRIENDS AND COMRADES CAME TO THE DOCKS TO SEE HER OFF... BUT ED BRADY WAS NOT AMONG THEM...
Dearest Brother Yegor,
As expected, my allowance
from Schmidt and Miller is far too
generous. They even gave me a gold
pocket watch for "Bon Voyage"! I
enclose a money order for your term's
fees at Medical School.
Can you still recall our Petersburg
winters? London's cold fogs are much
worse! The sky is dark at noon, and
the tiny fireplace is nothing like
our grand Russian stoves.
Patriotic frenzy whipped up
over the Boer War makes
for a chill climate for
dissent, as well.
Your loving
Emma

FIREBRAND
BRING THE TROOPS HOME
BRITAIN OUT OF SOUTH AFRICA
PEACE NOW
NO BLOOD FOR DIAMONDS
ON THIS SECOND TRIP TO STUDY IN EUROPE, EMMA NEVER GOT BACK TO MEDICAL SCHOOL. AFTER ONE OF HER ANTI-BOER WAR SPEECHES IN LONDON, AN AIMLESS CZECH GYPSY ANARCHIST INTRODUCED HIMSELF...
© Sharon Rudahl '06
HIPPOLYTE HAVEL, AT YOUR SERVICE!
BRING THE TROOPS HOME NOW
I'VE KEPT ALIVE WITH EVERY KIND OF DEGRADING WORK!
TAKE A LOOK AT MY HANDS!!
I'VE BEEN EXPELLED FROM EVERY COUNTRY IN EUROPE, AND IMPRISONED IN ALL THE GREAT CAPITALS!!
LABOR IS NOT DEGRADING.
HOW DID THIS HAPPEN?!?
EMMA NURSED AND FED HAVEL, AND SURRENDERED TO HER OWN COMPASSION...
THERE WAS SOMETHING STRANGE AND EXOTIC ABOUT THE MAN...
CLEANING BOOTS, CARRYING COALS, SCRUBBING FILTHY LINEN IN ICE-COLD WATER— WHAT CAN I DO, STATELESS, WITHOUT A TRADE?

EMMA WAS INVITED TO HELP ORGANIZE AN INTERNATIONAL ANARCHIST CONVENTION IN PARIS. SHE AND HAVEL CROSSED THE CHANNEL~
BILLETS
POSTE RESTANTE
MISS GOLDMAN? YES, THERE IS A LETTER FOR YOU...
Dear Miss Emma, I am not interested in funding old propaganda and a new lover. I am only interested in E.G. the woman. Please choose. Carl Schmidt
KEEP YOUR MONEY!!!
© Sharon Rudahl '06
HAVEL SPOKE FLUENT FRENCH AND KNEW THE BEST CHEAP CAFÉS. "HE MADE A PERFECT COMPANION."
EVERY STONE HAS ITS REVOLUTIONARY STORY, EVERY DISTRICT ITS HEROIC LEGEND!
BUT IN ENLIGHTENED FRANCE, THE ANARCHIST DELEGATES HAD TO MEET SECRETLY, ON THE OUTSKIRTS OF PARIS.
CANADA
UNITED STATES
COMRADES, I'VE BEEN ASKED TO SPEAK ABOUT ARRANGING A SUCCESSFUL PROPAGANDA TOUR...
IN PARIS, EMMA ALSO ATTENDED A COVERT NEO-MALTHUSIAN CONFERENCE, WHERE BIRTH CONTROL INFORMATION AND DEVICES WERE DISTRIBUTED.
FAMILY PLANNING
WITH COMSTOCK IN CHARGE OF MORALS IN THE U.S., YOU CAN'T EVEN DISCUSS THESE METHODS!
I KNOW MANY PEOPLE IN AMERICA BRAVE ENOUGH TO DO GOOD WORK...
TO MAKE ENDS MEET, EMMA AND HAVEL FREE-LANCED AS TOUR GUIDES, AND SOLD PREPARED MEALS TO HUNGRY ANARCHISTS AND NEO-MALTHUSIANS.
THAT'S ONE STUFFED CABBAGE, ONE NOODLE KUGEL, RIGHT?

SASHA BERKMAN WAS ALLOWED ONE LETTER PER MONTH FROM JAIL. IN PARIS, EMMA RECEIVED PROGRESS REPORTS ON HIS ESCAPE PLAN THRU NORWEGIAN COMRADE ERIK MORTEN.
"THE INVENTION IS PROGRESSING SLOWLY..."
WHAT IS IT ?!?
IN A FORTNIGHT, ERIK MORTEN SHOWED UP AT THEIR HOTEL IN THE MARAIS,
THE TUNNEL!! POLICE DISCOVERED "UN PASSAGE SOUTERRAIN" NEAR THE WESTERN PENITENTIARY!
EMMA!!
"THE BIG, STRONG VIKING HAD GROWN VERY THIN, HIS FACE ASHEN AND COVERED WITH BLISTERS."
TONY IS A CONCEITED FOOL!! HE REFUSED TO TEACH ME SASHA'S CIPHER, AND KEPT SHIFTING PLANS...
WE RENTED A HOUSE ACROSS FROM THE PRISON WALL, AND TUNNELED FROM THE CELLAR TOWARD THE CELL BLOCK OUTHOUSE...
LATRINES
SASHA'S CELL
WATCHTOWER III
CELLBLOCK A
BORDER STREET
ALLEY
BASEMENT
ROOMING HOUSE
GUARDHOUSE I
WE DUG AT NIGHT, WHILE A LADY FRIEND OF TONY'S PLAYED PIANO AND SANG TO COVER OUR NOISE...
NOXIOUS FUMES FILLED THE TUNNEL AND ALMOST KILLED US...
ON THE CHOSEN DAY, SASHA TORE UP THE ROTTING OUTHOUSE FLOOR BOARDS~
I WAS WAITING IN THE CELLAR WITH CLOTHES, MONEY, AND FORGED PAPERS...
© Sharon Rudahl '86

WE DUG ACCORDING TO TONY'S DIRECTIONS~ BUT THE TUNNEL CAME OUT IN THE WRONG PLACE, BLOCKED BY A PILE OF GRANITE CONSTRUCTION STONES!
LATRINES
BOARDER STREET
STERLING
PILE OF STONES
GUARDHOUSE
WATCHTOWER
AND SASHA?! IS HE ALIVE? WHAT DID THEY DO TO HIM???
BERKMAN GOT BACK TO HIS CELL. WE SEALED OFF THE BASEMENT ENTRANCE AND LEFT TOWN...
A FEW DAYS LATER, TWO BOYS STUMBLED INTO THE TUNNEL- BUT THE COPS ARE PINNING IT ON A NOTORIOUS GANG BOSS...
DECEMBER 1900 ~ EMMA AND HAVEL RETURNED TO THE U.S., HER MED STUDENT BROTHER YEGOR MET THEM AT THE DOCKS.
PAWN
EMMA PAWNED HER BON VOYAGE GIFT FROM SCHMIDT AND MILLER FOR A WEEK'S RENT.
SHE FOUND WORK NURSING A RECOVERING MORPHINE ADDICT- MRS. SPENCER, MADAM OF A HIGH-CLASS BROTHEL.
ARE YOU BY ANY CHANCE RELATED TO EMMA GOLDMAN, THE FAMOUS ANARCHIST?
I AM THE GUILTY PARTY!
MRS. SPENCER MADE A PET OF EMMA, AND BECAME DEPENDENT ON HER COMPANY.
DASHING ARMY OFFICER... OPERATION ALMOST KILLED ME... STRANDED IN EUROPE... WEALTHY POLITICIAN... MY HEALTH RUINED...
LET ME EXPLAIN THE SOCIAL FACTORS BEHIND YOUR OPPRESSION...
© Sharon Rudahl '06

MRS. SPENCER'S CURRENT PROTECTOR WAS A NOTORIOUS POLICE CAPTAIN.
THOSE DASTARDLY ANARCHISTS DON'T DARE SHOW THEIR FACES ON MY WATCH!!
OFFERED A JOB ON THE ANARCHIST PAPER NEW SOCIETY, HAVEL LEFT FOR CHICAGO... EMMA GREW IMPATIENT TO GET BACK ON THE LECTURE CIRCUIT...
NOW THAT YOU'RE OUT OF DANGER, I MUST TRY TO VISIT MY SWEETHEART — HE'S SERVING HARD TIME NEAR PITTSBURGH.
IF THEY WON'T LET ME SEE HIM, I'LL STAND OUTSIDE THE PRISON WALLS...
OF COURSE, DEAR, YOU MUST GO TO HIM! BUT HOW WILL I MANAGE WITHOUT YOU??
A LAW TAILORED TO AID TWO INFLUENTIAL TAX CHEATS HAD INADVERTENTLY RESTORED BERKMAN'S VISITING PRIVILEGES...
THIS WAS ONLY THE SECOND TIME SASHA AND EMMA HAD SEEN EACH OTHER SINCE THE ATTENTAT.
BERKMAN HAD JUST BEEN RELEASED FROM A LONG STINT IN SOLITARY. HE WAS UNABLE TO SAY A SINGLE WORD...
© Sharon Rudahl '06
A GREY MAN IN A GREY SUIT, SO SILENT AND THIN...
WAS WHAT WE DID WORTHWHILE? CAN THIS BE THE WAY TO THE GLORIOUS FUTURE WE IMAGINED???!

IN MAY 1901, EMMA SPOKE IN CLEVELAND. A YOUNG, UNEMPLOYED STEELWORKER CAME UP TO MEET HER...
STRIKE
COULD YOU PLEASE SUGGEST SOME BOOKS ABOUT ANARCHISM?
WHAT A HANDSOME, SENSITIVE FACE...
© Sharon Rudahl '06
LEON CZOLGOSZ HAD BEEN HANGING AROUND ANARCHIST CIRCLES IN THE MIDWEST. HE GAVE HIS NAME AS "NIEMAN" AND PROPOSED RISKY AND VIOLENT ACTIONS.
FREE SOCIETY
WORKER BEATEN
ATTENTION COMRADES! BE CAREFUL OF A MAN CALLING HIMSELF "NIEMAN." HE MAY BE A SPY OR AN AGENT PROVACATEUR. YOUR EDITOR, A. ISAAK
STRIKE DEADLINE
ON SEPTEMBER 6, 1901, AT THE PAN-AMERICAN EXPOSITION IN BUFFALO, NEW YORK, CZOLGOSZ SHOT PRESIDENT McKINLEY POINT-BLANK...
BANG
"MURDERER OF PRESIDENT CONFESSES—INCITED BY EMMA GOLDMAN"!
"EMMA GOLDMAN SET ME ON FIRE!!"
"HER LECTURE STARTED CRAZE TO KILL!!!"

IN THE HYSTERIA AFTER McKINLEY'S ASSASSINATION, VOLTAIRINE WAS ONE OF EMMA'S FEW DEFENDERS~
"THE WHOLE ATMOSPHERE IS SURCHARGED WITH BRUTALITY. ONE FEELS IN A DEN OF WILD BEASTS... I HAVE NEVER LIKED EMMA GOLDMAN, BUT I NEVER HEARD HER SAY ANYONE COULD DO ANY GOOD BY KILLING!!"
© Sharon Rudahl '06
HAVEL, ISAAK, AND TEN OTHERS FROM THE STAFF OF NEW SOCIETY WERE HELD WITHOUT BAIL IN CHICAGO. JOHANN MOST WAS JAILED FOR REPRINTING AN ARTICLE...
SASHA BERKMAN WENT BACK TO SOLITARY...
EMMA'S FAMILY WAS INTERROGATED, AND HER FATHER ABRAHAM EXPELLED FROM HIS SYNAGOGUE.
HER BELOVED NIECE STELLA GOT HARASSED AT HER SCHOOL~
YOUR AUNT KILLED OUR PRESIDENT!
GO BACK WHERE YOU CAME FROM!
EMMA MADE NO ATTEMPT TO HIDE FROM THE NATIONWIDE MANHUNT. SHE WENT TO CHICAGO TO GIVE HERSELF UP...
RECTORY
NO ONE WILL SUSPECT US OF SHELTERING THE TERRIBLE EMMA GOLDMAN!
DID YOU HEAR, THE CHICAGO TRIBUNE IS OFFERING $5,000 FOR AN INTERVIEW WITH YOU!?!
RECTORY
THAT $5,000 COULD GET SOME OF OUR COMRADES OUT OF JAIL- CAN YOU MAKE ARRANGEMENTS WITH THE TRIBUNE FOR ME?
THE POLICE DROVE UP JUST AHEAD OF THE REPORTERS. TO BUY TIME, EMMA PRETENDED TO BE THE MAID.
STAND BACK!!! WE'RE LOOKING FOR EMMA GOLDMAN!
PLEASE, TO WIPE MUDDY FEET, SIRS...

THIS WOMAN I NOT SEE — SHE LOOK MEAN!
EMMA GOLDMAN
WANTED
HEY! GET A LOAD OF THIS!!
Emma Goldman
"E-M-M-A ... G-O-L..." SHE MUSTA BEEN HERE!! MAYBE SHE'LL COME BACK!
EMMA HAD CARELESSLY LEFT OUT A GIFT FROM A FAN... THE JIG WAS UP.
I AM EMMA GOLDMAN.
THE CHICAGO POLICE GAVE HER THE THIRD DEGREE-
IN PAIN, A TOOTH KNOCKED LOOSE, EMMA WAS THROWN INTO COOK COUNTY JAIL-
LAST RESIDENCE OF THE HAYMARKET PRISONERS AWAITING EXECUTION ON TRUMPED-UP CHARGES.
TO KEEP UP HER SPIRITS, EMMA REPEATEDLY SANG A FAVORITE FOLK SONG OF HAYMARKET MARTYR ALBERT PARSONS...
"AND FOR BONNIE ANNIE LAURIE~ I'D LAY ME DOWN AND DIE..."
...AND NOW, THE END!! I'M ONLY 32, THERE'S STILL SO MUCH I HAVEN'T DONE...
© sharon Rudahl '06

from Miss Smith to MOTHER EARTH
THANKS TO A LOCAL FEUD, THE CHICAGO POLICE REFUSED TO EXTRADITE EMMA TO BUFFALO, NEW YORK.
BEATEN UNRECOGNIZABLE, CZOLGOSZ CONTINUED TO INSIST HE HAD ACTED ALONE.
EMMA GALLANTLY OFFERED TO NURSE THE DYING PRESIDENT, AND WAS PERMITTED TO ENTERTAIN GUESTS.
"NEWSPAPER PEOPLE CAME ALL DAY, NOT FOR INTERVIEWS BUT TO TALK, SMOKE, AND TELL FUNNY STORIES..."
AFTER DISRUPTING THE JAIL FOR A WEEK, EMMA WAS RELEASED, ALONG WITH HER FRIENDS HIPPOLYTE HAVEL AND A. ISAAK.
OF COURSE, IT'S A RELIEF TO BE FREE — BUT MY HEART GOES OUT TO THAT YOUNG MAN, ABOUT TO BE PUT TO DEATH.
CZOLGOSZ IS ONE OF THE DOWNTRODDEN WHO RESOLVE TO STRIKE A BLOW FOR THEIR FELLOW MEN. THE BLAME FOR SUCH ACTS MUST BE LAID AT THE DOOR OF THOSE RESPONSIBLE FOR INJUSTICE.
EMMA STOOD BY HERSELF IN DEFENDING McKINLEY'S ASSASSIN, THE FRIENDLESS SON OF POLISH IMMIGRANTS. SHE FAILED TO RAISE LEGAL FEES OR ORGANIZE SUPPORT MEETINGS.
WHY DO YOU SHIELD THAT BAD WOMAN EMMA GOLDMAN?
I DID IT ALONE, I DID IT FOR THE AMERICAN PEOPLE!!
ON OCTOBER 29, 1901, LEON CZOLGOSZ WAS EXECUTED.
HOUNDED BY THE AUTHORITIES, A PARIAH TO THE LEFT, EMMA LAID LOW, USING THE ALIAS "MISS SMITH."
MISS E.G. SMITH, WITH MY BROTHER IGOR – HE'S A MEDICAL STUDENT!
A MONTH DOWN, A MONTH IN ADVANCE, CASH, LADY...
ROOM FOR RENT
©Sharon Rudahl '06

By the early 20th century, most anarchists had rejected the romantic lure of individual acts of violence, embracing Kropotkin's vision of a cooperative mass movement. Even Sasha disowned Czolgosz–
"The social necessity for Leon's act was not manifest."
How can Sasha– himself misunderstood and repudiated– how can he misunderstand?
Over this dispute, Emma and Sasha broke contact for a year.
Emma withdrew from all social and political activity...
At least, let me treat you to a New Year's dinner!
I'm sorry, Ed, I'm just not up to it...
But Emma had to earn her living~
Of course, I will recommend "Miss Smith" as a private nurse!!
She turned to Solotaroff, her first friend in New York, now an eminent surgeon.
Miss E.G. Smith drudged in the tenements...
If I hadda hold of that godless Emma Goldman woman, I'd soak her in kerosene and burn her alive!
An organizer she had met in Europe invited Emma to speak to striking silk-weavers in New Jersey.
"I seized upon my first chance to speak after the Czolgosz tragedy as a desert wanderer falls upon a well..."
The night before her scheduled speech, Emma woke screaming...
The ghost of Czolgosz!!!
She cancelled her trip to New Jersey–
© Sharon Rudahl '06

IN 1902 A WAVE OF BRUTAL POGROMS AND PERSECUTIONS OF JEWS AND RADICALS IN RUSSIA AROUSED MASS PROTESTS IN NEW YORK. EMMA PARTICIPATED UNDER HER ASSUMED NAME.
NO MORE SIBERI
DOWN WITH THE CZAR
FREIHEIT
ARBEIT
OUR NEXT SPEAKER IS MISS E.G.SMITH~ THE ORGANIZER OF TODAY'S RALLY!
AT THE HEIGHT OF THE CZOLGOSZ HYSTERIA, SENATOR HAWLEY OFFERED $1,000.00 FOR A SHOT AT AN ANARCHIST~
DEAR SENATOR HAWLEY, PROVIDED YOU FIRST LET ME EXPLAIN THE PRINCIPLES OF ANARCHISM, I STAND READY TO TAKE YOUR SHOT, FREE OF CHARGE. VOLTAIRINE DE CLEYRE
VOLTAIRINE PUBLISHED THIS RESPONSE
WHEN VOLTAIRINE WAS SHOT BY A FORMER MUSIC PUPIL, MISS E.G.SMITH RAISED FUNDS FOR HER CARE.
McKINLEY'S VICE-PRESIDENT TEDDY ROOSEVELT TOOK OVER, AND THE U.S. ENTERED THE PROGRESSIVE ERA. MUCKRAKERS PRESSED FOR CORRECTIVE REFORMS, APPEALING TO U.S.-BORN INTELLECTUALS AND RESPECTABLE LIBERALS.
EMMA FOUND NEW FRIENDS AND ALLIES.
I DON'T WANT FINGERS IN MY SAUSAGE!!! HURRY UP AND PASS SOME FOOD AND DRUG LAWS!
YES, T.R.
The JUNGLE BY UPTON SINCLAIR
PERHAPS WE COULD PERSUADE MISS SMITH TO SPEAK AT OUR RALLY AGAINST CHILD LABOR?
HONORED, I'M SURE...
©Sharon Rudahl '06

I DO SO ENJOY YOUR MEETINGS! I LOVE SLUMMING!!
THE VERY PEOPLE WHO HAD BEEN HOSTILE TO EMMA BEGAN TO SEEK OUT MISS SMITH.
EMMA CORRESPONDED WITH SASHA AGAIN, NOW LESS THAN THREE YEARS FROM HIS RELEASE...
TO LIMIT ONESELF TO PROPAGANDA EXCLUSIVELY AMONG THE OPPRESSED DOES NOT ALWAYS BRING DESIRED RESULTS...
THE "ANTI-ANARCHIST" LAW WAS PASSED IN 1903, PROHIBITING U.S. ENTRY TO ANYONE OPPOSED TO ORGANIZED GOVERNMENT. THE LAW'S FIRST VICTIM WAS JOHN TURNER, AN ENGLISH ANARCHIST ON A SPEAKING TOUR. WITH HER NEW CONTACTS, EMMA ESTABLISHED A FREE SPEECH LEAGUE, FORERUNNER OF THE ACLU – the AMERICAN CIVIL LIBERTIES UNION.
MEETING TONITE – THE COOPER UNION
MISS E.G. SMITH: FREE JOHN TURNER
VOLTAIRINE DE CLEYRE: RIGHT TO SPEECH
JOHN TURNER IS BEING HELD ON ELLIS ISLAND IN A 9'X6' CAGE FOR SIMPLY SAYING WHAT HE THINKS!
FREE SPEECH MEANS NOTHING IF IT DOES NOT MEAN THE FREEDOM TO SAY WHAT OTHERS DON'T WANT TO HEAR!
THOSE WHO WORKED CLOSELY WITH EMMA KNEW HER DUAL IDENTITY. A FREQUENT ALLY WAS LIBERTARIAN LAWYER BOLTON HALL.
CAN WE GET CLARENCE DARROW TO HANDLE THE TURNER APPEAL?
CONSIDER IT DONE, EMMA, DEAR...
WHEN YET ANOTHER NERVOUS LANDLORD EVICTED EMMA, BOLTON BOUGHT HER A LITTLE FARM RETREAT UP THE HUDSON RIVER...
© Sharon Rudahl '06

ON TOUR GIVING LECTURES FOR THE FREE SPEECH LEAGUE, EMMA VISITED HER SISTER HELENA IN ROCHESTER...
TANTE EMMA!
MY ARRIVAL WAS THE OCCASION FOR A GENERAL FAMILY REUNION.
INFORMED THAT "MISS SMITH" WAS HIS OLD EMPLOYEE EMMA GOLDMAN, GARMENT FACTORY BOSS GARSON INVITED HER TO HIS OFFICE.
WHO WOULD HAVE THOUGHT MY LITTLE SHOPGIRL WOULD BECOME A FAMOUS SPEAKER??
WHAT DO YOU WANT?
NAME YOUR OWN PRICE, JUST PERSUADE MY WORKERS TO SEE MY SIDE, A LITTLE-
YOU'VE COME TO THE WRONG PERSON, MR. GARSON. YOU CAN'T BUY EMMA GOLDMAN!
SHE RETURNED TO THE PENNSYLVANIA MINE WHERE A STRIKE HAD BEEN "SETTLED" FIVE YEARS EARLIER...
A MAN OF NINETY AND A CHILD OF EIGHT WORK TEN HOURS A DAY IN A BLACK PIT.
© Sharon Rudahl '06
CATHERINE "BABUSHKA" BRESHKOVSKAYA, THE GRANDMOTHER OF THE RUSSIAN REVOLUTION, STUMPED NEW YORK HOPING TO RAISE FUNDS. HER SUPPORTERS ON THE LOWER EAST SIDE PRESSED "MISS SMITH" INTO SERVICE AS HOSTESS AND TRANSLATOR.
FRIENDS OF RUSSIAN FREEDOM
DOWN WITH THE CZAR
ЗДРáВСТВУЙ ТЕ!
СПАСИ́БО
ERIK THE VIKING, TUNNEL BUILDER FOR SASHA'S FAILED JAILBREAK, MANAGED TO SMUGGLE "BABUSHKA" BACK TO RUSSIA JUST IN TIME FOR THE 1905 REVOLUTION.
LAND REFORM! CIVIL RIGHTS! A NATIONAL ASSEMBLY!!
The New York Times
RUSSIAN CZAR CONCEDES GENERAL STRI
DUMA ELECTED

THE DISASTROUS RUSSO-JAPANESE WAR LED TO A FIRST, FAILED REVOLUTION. AFTER 1905, RUSSIA WAS GOVERNED BY AN INEFFECTUAL CONGRESS CALLED THE DUMA. FACTIONS SQUABBLED AND THE COUNTRY SPIRALED DOWN INTO CONDITIONS RIPE FOR THE 1917 BOLSHEVIK REVOLUTION.
IN NEW YORK, EMMA WAS EXHAUSTED BY HER EFFORTS AS MISS SMITH, FED UP WITH WORKING NIGHTS AS A PRIVATE NURSE TO PAY THE BILLS...
BOLTON, WHAT WOULD YOU THINK OF MY OPENING A THERAPEUTIC FACIAL AND SCALP MASSAGE PARLOR?
FOR RENT
I'LL LEND YOU THE MONEY TO GET STARTED...
EVEN IF YOUR SKILL WON'T BRING BACK MY HAIR, I'LL HAVE YOU PINNED DOWN FOR AN HOUR TO LISTEN TO MY ARGUMENTS ON THE SINGLE TAX!!
EMMA NOW HAD A STABLE RESIDENCE, AT 210 EAST 13TH St., AND HER NIECE STELLA CAME TO LIVE WITH HER~
THERE'S NO WORK IN ROCHESTER BUT THE MILLS... I PROMISE NOT TO GET IN YOUR WAY...
I'VE LONGED FOR THIS DAY SINCE YOU WERE A BABY!!!
©Sharon Rudahl 06
TANTE EMMA!! CAN YOU BELIEVE IT?!? I GOT HIRED AS SECRETARY TO A DISTRICT JUDGE!
HE'LL DIE OF HORROR IF HE FINDS OUT YOU'RE EMMA GOLDMAN'S NIECE!!
THE MASSAGE PARLOR FLOURISHED...
EMMA FACE & SCALP MASSAGE
MASSAGE
BUT EMMA DROPPED EVERYTHING TO RESCUE AN AVANT-GARDE RUSSIAN THEATRE TROUPE.
STRANDED PENNILESS IN NEW YORK!
PAVEL ORLENOFF PLAYERS present THE CHOSEN PEOPLE
I TAKE THIS PLAY ABROAD AS PROTEST AGAINST POGROMS IN RUSSIA!!

THESE BARBARIANS DO NOT UNDERSTAND THEATER FOR THE PEOPLE!!
OUR ART IS TOO DEEP FOR THEM, PAVEL DARLING...
UNDER THE DEVOTED MANAGEMENT OF MISS E.G. SMITH, PAVEL ORLENOFF AND HIS STAR NAZIMOVA ENJOYED A SUCCESSFUL SEASON.
NOTHING LIKE THEIR ACTING HAS EVER BEEN SEEN ON THE AMERICAN STAGE!
NAZIMOVA LATER WON FAME FOR HER SILENT MOVIE SALOMÉ.
STELLA GOT A PERMIT FROM HER JUDGE FOR THE ENTIRE COMPANY TO CAMP ON HUNTERS ISLAND.
WE ESCAPE STIFLING, ARTIFICIAL CITY!!
ALSO, IS NO RENT!
WHEN POISON IVY AND MOSQUITOES DROVE THEM BACK INTO MANHATTAN, MISS SMITH DRUMMED UP WEALTHY PATRONS. A DERELICT THEATER ON 3RD ST WAS REFURBISHED. EVEN JANE ADDAMS AND THE BARRYMORES VIED FOR TICKETS...
CRIME AND PUNISHMENT
STARRING NAZIMOVA
ORLENOFF PLAYHOUSE
THEY COULD MAKE MORE MONEY IF THEY PUT ON PLAYS WITH HAPPY ENDINGS.
EVERYTHING YOU HAVE DONE FOR US... NOW IS TIME WE DO FOR YOU...
...IS TIME YOU WRITE IN OWN NAME, OWN VOICE!
MY WORK OF YEARS PUT DOWN IN LASTING FORM?!
PAVEL INTERPRETED IBSEN AND STRINDBERG. NAZIMOVA DESIGNED DAZZLING SETS AND COSTUMES.
ORLENOFF PROPOSED A SERIES OF BENEFIT PERFORMANCES TO FINANCE PUBLICATION OF EMMA'S OWN MAGAZINE.
A MAGAZINE COMBINING MY SOCIAL IDEAS WITH AN OUTLET FOR FREE EXPRESSION IN ART AND LITERATURE!
©Sharon Rudahl

HIPPOLYTE HAVEL CAME BACK FROM CHICAGO TO WORK ON EMMA'S MAGAZINE, WITH OLD CHUM MAX BAGINSKI AND SELF-TAUGHT PRINTER HARRY KELLY...
I WANT IT TO BE CALLED THE OPEN ROAD, AFTER THE WALT WHITMAN POEM...
COPYRIGHT PROBLEMS THERE, I'M AFRAID...
THEN, LET'S CALL IT— MOTHER EARTH...
MOTHER EARTH, THE NOURISHER OF FREE MAN!!
WHEN THE CURTAIN CAME DOWN ON ORLENOFF'S FIRST BENEFIT PERFORMANCE, A SWARM OF CREDITORS HAD HIM ARRESTED—
NO ENTRY BY ORDER OF N.Y.C.
TICKETS
CLOSED
ORLENOFF presents
CANCELLED
MOTHER EARTH
MARCH 1906
BUT THERE WAS ENOUGH MONEY IN THE TILL TO FUND THE FIRST ISSUE OF MOTHER EARTH.
DISPATCHES FROM THE MEXICAN REVOLUTION!
A SCENE FROM THE LATEST LITTLE THEATER PRODUCTION!
VOLTAIRINE ON SEX SLAVERY AND AMERICAN HISTORY!
THE INFORMAL PUBLISHING COLLECTIVE WORKED OUT OF 210 E. 13TH, WITH EMMA SLEEPING IN AN ALCOVE BEHIND THE FLAT FILES... FROM 1906-1917, READERSHIP RANGED FROM 4,000-10,000, MOSTLY NATIVE-BORN DISSIDENTS AND ASPIRING IMMIGRANTS.
NIETZSCHE, DOSTOIEVSKY, PROUDHON...
THOREAU, DREISER, EMERSON...
POEMS THAT RHYME, NOTHING IN STREAM OF CONSCIOUSNESS!
NOT ENOUGH REVOLUTIONARY THEORY!
POEMS, SHORT STORIES, ESSAYS, CARTOONS!
MOTHER EARTH
JUST WHAT WE NEEDED!
NEVER THE CUTTING EDGE IN MODERN LITERATURE, MOTHER EARTH WAS VERY MUCH EMMA'S BABY, A BRIDGE BETWEEN EUROPEAN ENLIGHTENMENT AND NEW WORLD SOCIAL ACTIVISM.

TWO MONTHS AFTER THE FIRST ISSUE OF MOTHER EARTH WAS PUBLISHED, ... ALEXANDER BERKMAN WALKED OUT OF THE WORKHOUSE A FREE MAN...
DETROIT
WELCO
SASH
WHY, IT'S THE GIRL!! HOW LITTLE SHE'S CHANGED!
THAT STRANGE-LOOKING MAN– HIS HAT TOO BIG, HIS FACE DEATHLY WHITE – WAS THAT SASHA??
... I WAS SEIZED WITH TERROR AND PITY...
© Sharon Rudahl '00

SASHA WAS INCARCERATED A YOUTH OF 21, RELEASED PREMATURELY OLD AT 35...
...AT LAST, SASHA AND I WERE ALONE. WE LOOKED AT EACH OTHER LIKE CHILDREN LEFT ALONE IN THE DARK...
I'D LIKE TO GO OUT FOR A WALK. THE WALLS ARE CRUSHING ME...
© Sharon Rudahl '06
IN PRISON, SASHA HAD EDUCATED HIMSELF. CONTACT WITH SOCIETY'S REJECTS HAD REFINED HIS POLITICAL IDEAS. BUT ORDINARY HOPES AND DESIRES HAD BEEN CRUSHED OUT OF HIM...
SASHA ATE RAVENOUSLY, IT WAS EXTRAORDINARY HOW MUCH HE COULD ABSORB.
WHEN HE WAS NOT EATING, HE ROAMED THE WOODS OR LAY STRETCHED ON THE GROUND, SILENT AND LISTLESS.
I MUST FIND WORK TO OCCUPY MY MIND— OR I WILL GO MAD.
COME BACK TO EAST 13TH WITH ME ~ HELP EDIT MOTHER EARTH!
EMMA TOOK HIM TO HER COUNTRY PLACE UP THE HUDSON AND FATTENED HIM UP ON BLINTZES AND STUFFED CABBAGE...
ED BRADY HAD BEEN FELLED BY A HEART ATTACK AT THE TIME OF THE FREE SPEECH CAMPAIGN. JOHANN MOST DIED ON A LECTURE TOUR THE MONTH MOTHER EARTH CAME OUT. EMMA'S OTHER LOVE AFFAIRS HAD SETTLED INTO FRIENDSHIPS. SHE EXPECTED TO RESUME LIFE WITH SASHA. BUT THEY WERE NEVER AGAIN PHYSICALLY LOVERS...
MY LITTLE SAILOR HAS BECOME A WOMAN OF THE WORLD!!
MOTHER EARTH
SAN DIEGO EDITION
MOTHER EARTH
October, 19.
YOU HAVE YOUR OWN CAREER NOW, EMMA. YOU DON'T NEED ME.
COMRADES IN THE MIDWEST ARE BEGGING YOU TO SPEAK ABOUT PRISON CONDITIONS. HOW ABOUT ABOUT A SHORT LECTURE TOUR?
WESTERN UNION
AFTER FIRST MEETING BERKMAN MISSING STOP PLEASE ADVISE STOP NISSAKI
THE NIGHT SASHA WAS SCHEDULED TO SPEAK IN CLEVELAND, EMMA RECEIVED A TELEGRAM.

EXTRA!!!
The World
RECENTLY FREED ANARCHIST DISAPPEARS
AFTER THREE DAYS AND NIGHTS, SASHA CONTACTED EMMA VIA A YOUNG COMRADE—
EVEN THE DETECTIVE ASSIGNED TO KEEP TRACK OF SASHA HASN'T GOT A CLUE... ANY NEWS HERE, STELLA??
BECKY EDELSON JUST CALLED - SASHA WANTS TO MEET YOU AT THE CAFE ON EAST 14TH!!!
©Sharon Rudahl '06
AT MY FIRST SPEECH, THE HALL WAS HALF EMPTY. NO ONE SEEMED INTERESTED IN WHAT I SAID...I DREADED FACING ANOTHER AUDIENCE...
I AWOKE IN THE MIDDLE OF THE NIGHT, WALKED INTO CLEVELAND, AND BOUGHT A REVOLER...
I ROAMED FOR THREE DAYS WITHOUT EATING OR SLEEPING. BUT I KEPT HEADING BACK TOWARD NEW YORK...
THIS MORNING I SAW LITTLE CHILDREN IN THE PARK, AND REMEMBERED THE PAST—
... AND THEN I KNEW I COULDN'T DIE WITHOUT SEEING YOU AGAIN...

FROM THE 1880S, U.S. LABOR UNIONS WERE ON THE **RISE**... THE **AMERICAN FEDERATION OF LABOR** REPRESENTED SKILLED WORKERS. IN 1905, THE **INDUSTRIAL WORKERS OF THE WORLD** UNITED THE UNSKILLED, IMMIGRANTS, MIGRATORY WORKERS, EVEN **HOBOS** ~ MEN AND WOMEN OF ALL RACES ~ INTO "**ONE BIG UNION.**" THE WOBBLIES' AIMS WERE **REVOLUTIONARY,** THEIR METHOD **DIRECT ACTION**. THOUGH ANARCHISTS WERE WARY OF ORGANIZATIONS, THEY EMBRACED THE I.W.W.

KING OF THE HOBOS

DURING HIS PRISON YEARS, SASHA ABANDONED **INDIVIDUAL** ACTS OF PROTEST IN FAVOR OF **ALLIANCE** WITH **LABOR.** EMMA TURNED TO CULTURAL AND PERSONAL **LIBERATION**...

WE DID NOT HAVE A SINGLE THOUGHT IN COMMON... YET I FELT BOUND TO SASHA **FOREVER** BY THE TEARS AND BLOOD OF 14 YEARS...

A CRACKDOWN BY NEW YORK'S NEWLY FORMED **ANARCHIST SQUAD** AWOKE SASHA FROM HIS STUPOR ~

THE **COPS** BROKE UP OUR RALLY!! THEY **ARRESTED** MY BROTHER AND EMMA!!!

DON'T **WORRY**, BECKY, BOLTON WILL GET THEM OUT!

THE ADMIRATION OF 15 YEAR OLD BECKY **ALSO** HELPED RESTORE SASHA'S **CONFIDENCE**...
WE'LL CALL A **PROTEST MEETING!**
"CRIMINAL ANARCHY" CHARGES AGAINST EMMA AND BECKY'S BROTHER WERE **DROPPED.** BUT THE ANARCHIST SQUAD SUPPRESSED ALL PROGRESSIVE ORGANIZING, EVEN RAIDING A MASKED BALL **FUNDRAISER** FOR MOTHER EARTH.

I HAVE TO GO BACK ON TOUR, TO RAISE MONEY TO KEEP THE MAGAZINE AFLOAT...
WOULD YOU BE WILLING TO TAKE CHARGE OF MOTHER EARTH WHILE I'M OUT OF TOWN?
ARE YOU JUST TRYING TO KEEP ME OCCUPIED?!?
GIVING SPEECHES AND SELLING SUBSCRIPTIONS TO MOTHER EARTH, EMMA'S PLANNED 16 WEEK TOUR STRETCHED INTO NINE MONTHS-
©Sharon Rudahl '08
THEN SHE AND COLLEAGUE MAX BAGINSKI WERE INVITED TO AMSTERDAM.
WE'VE BEEN ASKED TO REPRESENT THE U.S. AT THE INTERNATIONAL ANARCHIST CONGRESS!... I'LL SEND BACK REPORTS FOR MOTHER EARTH!!
VIENNA
LONDON
PARIS
YOU'RE DOING A GREAT JOB HERE AS EDITOR-IN-CHIEF!
EMMA, MY HEART ISN'T IN MOTHER EARTH... I WANT TO PUT OUT A WEEKLY PROPAGANDA PAPER FOR WORKERS...
BUT I'LL WAIT TILL YOU GET BACK FROM EUROPE.
IN 1907, ANARCHISTS FROM ALL OVER THE WORLD MET OPENLY IN MONARCHICAL HOLLAND...
ANARCHISM DOES NOT REQUIRE A CHOICE BETWEEN IBSEN'S INDIVIDUALISM AND KROPOTKIN'S MUTUAL AID- IT EMBRACES BOTH.

STELLA JOINED EMMA IN PARIS, WHERE THEY TOURED THE CONFEDERATION DU TRAVAIL, A COMMUNITY CENTER ESTABLISHED BY ANARCHIST WORKERS.
THE WORKERS THEMSELVES RUN THE CLINIC, NIGHT CLASSES, PRINTING SHOP, INFANT NURSERY...
THEY VISITED LA RUCHE - THE BEEHIVE - A HIPPIE-STYLE REFUGE FOR ORPHANS.
"SCHOOL IS FOR THE CHILD WHAT PRISON IS TO THE CONVICT AND THE BARRACKS FOR THE SOLDIER..."
WE SHOULD FEEL AT FAULT WERE THE CHILDREN TO HONOR US MERELY BECAUSE WE ARE THEIR ELDERS...
©Sharon Rudahl '06
EFFORTS WERE ALREADY UNDERWAY TO ANNUL EMMA'S U.S. CITIZENSHIP. WARNED THAT THE ANTI-ANARCHIST ACT MIGHT BE USED TO BAR HER REENTRY, SHE AND STELLA SAILED FROM LIVERPOOL TO CANADA...
PLEASE WAKE ME UP WHEN WE REACH NEW YORK CITY, PORTER...
...THEN TOOK THE TRAIN FROM MONTREAL TO GRAND CENTRAL STATION.
BARELY 5 WEEKS AFTER HER RETURN FROM EUROPE, EMMA LEFT SASHA IN CHARGE OF MOTHER EARTH AND WENT BACK ON TOUR.
IWW
IWW
ONE BIG UNION
FREE BILL HAYWOOD
THE NEW FORMS OF LIFE WILL TAKE THE PLACE OF THE OLD NOT BY PREACHING OR VOTING BUT BY LIVING THEM!!
THE WINTER OF 1908, THOUSANDS IN EVERY U.S. CITY WERE OUT OF WORK AND IN MISERY. POLICE ATTACKED DEMONSTRATORS, SHOT STRIKERS, AND ARRESTED AGITATORS, INCLUDING VOLTAIRINE.
THIS VICIOUS CRACKDOWN ESPECIALLY TARGETED THE SPREADING INFLUENCE OF THE I.W.W.
CHICAGO
YOU'D BEST GET BACK ON THE TRAIN, SISTER! POLICE WON'T LET YOU SPEAK, HERE!
I WILL STAY IN CHICAGO AND FIGHT FOR OUR RIGHT TO BE HEARD!

IN CHICAGO, EVERY STEP EMMA TOOK WAS SHADOWED. THREATENED LANDLORDS REFUSED TO RENT HER A HALL...
TILLIE'S
THAT'S DR. BEN'S STOREFRONT, DOWN BY THE WHARF...
TILLIE'S
ROOMS $1/NT $3/WK $5 WITH BOARD
DR. REITMAN SAYS YOU'RE WELCOME TO GIVE SPEECHES AT HIS HOBO HALL!
JUST LAST WEEK, POLICE KNOCKED THE BEJESUS OUT OF BEN FOR LEADING THE UNEMPLOYED MARCH!
I'M SURPRISED DR. BEN'S STILL LOOKING FOR TROUBLE!
YOU KNOW BEN, HE'S ALWAYS LOOKING FOR TROUBLE!!
THE "KING OF THE HOBOS" SHOWED UP AT TILLIE'S THAT AFTERNOON~
SO THIS IS THE LITTLE LADY, EMMA GOLDMAN! I'VE ALWAYS WANTED TO KNOW YOU!!
A PICTURESQUE FIGURE, WITH A LARGE BLACK COWBOY HAT AND FLOWING SILK TIE... A MASS OF UNWASHED BLACK CURLY HAIR, HUGE DREAMY BROWN EYES, FULL PASSIONATE LIPS...
© Sharon Rudahl '06

DR. BEN REITMAN
TEN YEARS YOUNGER THAN EMMA, BEN WAS THE CONVERTED SON OF JEWISH IMMIGRANTS. AT THE AGE OF 11, HE RAN AWAY FROM HOME, RODE THE RAILS, WORKED ON A TRAMP STEAMER, AND WASHED BOTTLES FOR A DOCTOR WHO URGED HIM TO ENTER MEDICAL SCHOOL.
DR. REITMAN TREATED THE VICTIMS OF THE SAN FRANCISCO EARTHQUAKE. HE ORGANIZED THE CHICAGO-BASED HOBO COLLEGE, WHICH PROVIDED FOOD, HOUSING, AND MEDICAL CARE TO THE UNEMPLOYED.
"THERE WAS NO TIME IN MY LIFE WHEN I DID NOT KNOW DRUNKARDS, PIMPS AND WHORES, BEGGARS AND CROOKS..."
HOBO HALL
BEN'S HOBOS CLEANED UP THE STORE FRONT, CONSTRUCTED BENCHES, AND BUILT A SPEAKER'S PLATFORM FOR EMMA.
DEPT. OF BUILDING AND SAFETY—
WE'LL HAVE TO SHUT YOU DOWN!!
THIS SITE IS NOT SAFE FOR OCCUPATION!!
SO YOU CAN'T MEET AT BEN'S?! IF YOU WANT TO ATTRACT ALL THE LOCAL RIFFRAFF, JUST OFFER FREE FOOD AND DRINKS...
...WE COULD PUT ON A SOCIAL, AND I'LL SHOW UP LATE AND GIVE MY SPEECH!!
SOCIAL
REFRESHMENTS
MUSIC
FREE
SAT 8PM
AND NOW A FAMOUS FRIEND OF THE PEOPLE WILL ADDRESS OUR GATHERING!
YER UNDER ARREST!
BUT WHEN EMMA SLIPPED IN THE BACK DOOR, REPORTERS AND DETECTIVES WERE WAITING FOR HER ...
©Sharon Rudahl '06

THE POLICE WANT TO START ANOTHER HAYMARKET RIOT— DON'T GIVE THEM ANY EXCUSE!!
SOMEBODY MUSTA TIPPED OFF THE NEWSBOYS AND THE COPS!
MY MONEY'S ON BEN... HE HASN'T SHOWN HIS FACE SINCE THE SOCIAL...
Chicago Tribune
ANARCHISTS MEET AT TILLIE'S TAVERN
EMMA GOLDMAN WINS RELEASE
DR. BEN'S WAITING FOR YOU AT THE OYSTER BAR ON STATE STREET.
DR. REITMAN'S HOBO AIDE BROUGHT EMMA A MESSAGE~
HOWDY, DR. BEN!
HOW'S TRICKS, HOBO BEN?!
TORN BETWEEN SUSPICION AND SHAMEFUL ATTRACTION, EMMA LEFT CHICAGO WITHOUT TALKING TO DR. REITMAN.
...IN MILWAUKEE, THE NEXT STOP ON HER TOUR...
HOTEL
MISS GOLDMAN? TELEGRAM FOR YOU M'AM...
THANK YOU...
"I LOVE YOU. I WANT YOU. PLEASE LET ME JOIN YOU~ BEN"
WESTERN UNION
THE OUTCASTS DEPEND ON ME WHEN THEY'RE IN TROUBLE— I HAVE TO KEEP ON GOOD TERMS WITH THE POLICE!
EMMA WIRED BACK: "COME"
© Sharon Rudahl '06

THUS BEGAN THEIR TEN YEAR PATTERN OF ANGRY PARTINGS AND ECSTACTIC REUNIONS...
PLEASE BELIEVE ME AND LET ME PROVE MY LOVE FOR YOU...
"I WAS CAUGHT IN THE GRIP OF AN ELEMENTAL PASSION I NEVER DREAMED ANY MAN COULD ROUSE IN ME—
I RESPONDED SHAMELESSLY TO ITS PRIMITIVE BEAUTY, ITS ECSTATIC JOY..."
EMMA GOLDMAN TO-DAY
EMMA GOLDMAN SPECIAL
Albert Hall
SPECTACLE PRODUCTIONS
Orpheum
ODEON
WITH BEN AS MY MANAGER, MY WORK WAS LIFTED OUT OF ITS FORMER NARROW CONFINES
FEARED BY THE CROWNED HEADS OF EUROPE, TERROR OF THE NEW YORK CONSTABULARY...
... BOOKINGS INTO THEATERS, CHURCHES, LODGEHALLS, UNIVERSITIES— I'LL GET THE HANDBILLS TO THE PRINTER TONITE!
BEN WAS TYPICALLY AMERICAN IN HIS LOVE OF PUBLICITY AND SHOW
BEN TOOK OVER AS EMMA'S AGENT AND IMPRESARIO...
HE BOUGHT DISPLAY ADS IN THE POPULAR PRESS, ALERTED REPORTERS AND WARMED UP THE AUDIENCE BEFORE EMMA APPEARED.
EMMA AND BEN SPENT MOST OF EACH YEAR TOGETHER ON THE ROAD, HITTING AS MANY AS 37 CITIES IN 25 STATES.
Every nerve is tense, my t— is hot & burning my m— scream with delight. I want to f— you Love, Mommy
DR. REITMAN WAS EMMA'S DEMON LOVER, GIVING FULL MEASURE OF THE DARK SIDE OF FREE LOVE—JEALOUSY, HUMILIATION, SCREAMING FIGHTS, LIES...
WHILE THEY WERE APART, EMMA WROTE TORRID LETTERS, INDICATING COARSE WORDS WITH INITIALS...
©Sharon Rudahl '06

BEN WAS A COMPULSIVE WOMANIZER WHO HAD ALREADY ABANDONED ONE FAMILY. HE WAS EXCESSIVELY DEVOTED TO HIS MOTHER AND NOT ABOVE DIPPING HIS HAND INTO THE LECTURE TOUR TILL...
BEN HAD PROFOUND SYMPATHY FOR SOCIETY'S REJECTS BUT NO REAL SOCIAL CONSCIOUSNESS.
BUT IN HER YEARS WITH DR. REITMAN, EMMA ENJOYED NOT ONLY HER MOST FULFILLING SEX BUT THE MOST PRODUCTIVE AND CELEBRATED PERIOD OF HER CAREER.
EVERYONE IS AN ANARCHIST AT HEART... ALL THE PEOPLE WALKING DOWN 2ND AVE — ONLY THEY DON'T KNOW IT!
LIFE TAKES ON AN INTENSER QUALITY IN HER PRESENCE!
SHE HAS THE VOICE OF THE ANGEL GABRIEL!!
YOU AND ME, MY BLUE-EYED MOMMY...
IN 1908 EMMA AND BEN WERE ARRESTED ON TOUR IN SEATTLE, THEIR MEETINGS IN OHIO AND MICHIGAN WERE LOCKED OUT BY THE COPS.
AT THIS TIME THE U.S. WAS EMBROILED IN COLONIAL ADVENTURES IN THE PACIFIC. WHEN EMMA CAME TO SAN FRANCISCO TO SPEAK ON THE TOPIC OF PATRIOTISM, SHE WAS MET BY THE CHIEF OF POLICE.
...IS IT TRUE MISS GOLDMAN, YOU'VE COME TO BLOW UP THE AMERICAN FLEET IN OUR HARBOUR?
WHY WASTE A BOMB? I HAVE COME TO POINT OUT THE USELESSNESS AND WASTE OF MILITARY INSTITUTIONS!
MOUNTED TROOPERS LINED THE STREETS.
U.S. OUT OF THE PHILIPPINES
DOWN WITH DOLLAR DIPLOMACY
PATRIOTISM IS THE EXCUSE USED TO JUSTIFY THE TRAINING OF WHOLESALE MURDERERS!!
THANK YOU FOR SPEAKING, MISS GOLDMAN...
WILLIAM BUWALDA, A PRIVATE STATIONED AT THE PRESIDIO, WAS SENTENCED TO 5 YEARS ON ALCATRAZ FOR SHAKING EMMA'S HAND...
PARDONED AFTER 10 MONTHS, HE TURNED IN HIS MEDALS AND JOINED THE ANARCHISTS.
BEFORE LEAVING CALIFORNIA, EMMA AND BEN SPENT 3 DAYS DRINKING AND ARGUING WITH JACK LONDON AT GLEN ELLEN.
@#☆!!
© Sabrina Jones '06

BACK IN NEW YORK, THE ANARCHIST SQUAD BROKE UP EMMA'S SUNDAY MORNING THEATER LECTURE— ONE OF A PROFITABLE SERIES DREAMED UP BY BEN...
IBSEN IS THE UNCOMPROMISING DEMOLISHER OF ALL FALSE IDOLS—
YER UNDER ARREST!!
SHE AND SASHA WERE BRIEFLY HELD FOR "INCITING TO RIOT"— BUT THE CRACK-DOWN ON IBSEN WON THE SUPPORT OF PATRONS OF THE ARTS.
HOW DARE THEY SUPPRESS THE FATHER OF MODERN DRAMA!
PLEASE ACCEPT OUR DONATION FOR YOUR FREE SPEECH SOCIETY!
THE NEW YORK WORLD PUBLISHED EMMA'S "WHAT I BELIEVE," PAYING HER ENOUGH TO CLEAR MOTHER EARTH'S PRINTING BILL AND BRING BEN TO NEW YORK...
BEN ACTED LIKE A CHILD EXPECTED TO BE ON GOOD BEHAVIOUR...
MOTHER EARTH
I FELT ASHAMED OF HIM AND RESENTFUL OF MY FRIENDS...
HOW CAN YOU LOVE SUCH A MAN?? HE DOES NOT BELONG IN OUR MOVEMENT!!!
EEEEP
WHY SHOULD PEOPLE STANDING FOR FREEDOM OBJECT TO SOMEONE BEHAVING NATURALLY?
BUT I WAS ENTHRALLED BY THIS LIVING EMBODIMENT OF A CHARACTER FROM GORKY OR DOSTOYEVSKY.
EMMA WENT BACK ON THE ROAD WITH BEN, PRESSING THE FREE SPEECH CAMPAIGN.
I BELIEVE THAT FREE SPEECH MEANS THAT I MAY SAY AND WRITE WHAT I PLEASE!
TERRORIST!!
FREE LOVER!
SAW 'ER LOOSE AFORE SHE STARTS A RIOT!!
THIS WAS THE HEYDAY OF THE IWW. FRESH FROM VICTORIES IN THE MCKEE'S STEEL AND LAWRENCE MILL WORKERS' STRIKES, MIGRANT IWWS SPREAD THEIR MESSAGE TO THE WEST COAST—
THE COPPERS NAILED OUR FELLAS IN PORTLAND!
GET THE WORD OUT!! HELP US FILL THE JAILS!
© Sharon Rudahl '06

WHEREVER IWW RABBLE ROUSING WAS SHUT DOWN, WOBBLIES POURED IN TO CROWD THE JAILS, OVERWHELMING THE FORCES OF LAW AND ORDER...
SOLIDARITY FOREVER!!
SOL-I-DAR-ITY FOREVER!
SOLIDARITY FOR-EVER!
MAY 1912—IWW MEETINGS IN SAN DIEGO WERE BRUTALLY SUPPRESSED, RESULTING IN THE DEATH OF ONE YOUNG WOBBLY.
EMMA AND BEN ARRIVED TO LEAD THE FUNERAL PROCESSION.
WE WERE ALL FORCED TO KNEEL AND KISS THE FLAG...
THEN THE PIGS CLOBBERED US WITH CLUBS AND BLACKJACKS
AT THE GRAVEYARD, MEN IN HOODS GRABBED BEN AND EMMA AND FORCED THEM INTO SEPARATE CARS...
BEN'S KIDNAPPERS DROVE OUT INTO THE DESERT...
I CHARGE ALL YOU MEN WITH BEING IN LEAGUE WITH THE VIGILANTES!!
MAYOR
POLICE CHIEF
EMMA WAS CONFINED IN THE LUXURIOUS U.S. GRANT HOTEL...
THERE HE WAS TORTURED, SEXUALLY ABUSED AND BRANDED ON HIS BUTTOCKS.
AT MIDNIGHT, THE SAN DIEGO CITY FATHERS PUT DOWN THEIR CARDS AND LEFT THE HOTEL...
TICK
TOCK
IF YOU WANT TO SEE YOUR PAL AGAIN, STAY PUT AND SHUT UP!!
IWW
© Sharon Rudahl '06

RING
RING
RING
IN SPITE OF BEN'S PLEADING, EMMA CONTINUED HER SCHEDULED LECTURE TOUR...
DR. REITMAN IS BOARDING A TRAIN TO LA... HIS FRIENDS SHOULD BRING A STRETCHER -
IS HE ALIVE?!?
OH, MOMMY, I'M WITH YOU AT LAST... TAKE ME AWAY, TAKE ME HOME...
NOTE FOR YOU, MIZ GOLDMAN...
WHEN YOU ENTER THE HALL YOU WILL BE SHOT!
IF ONLY I CAN PROTECT MY FACE!!
©Sharon Rudahl '06
EMMA DELIVERED HER SPEECH WITHOUT INCIDENT..
IT'S A SHOCK TO DISCOVER IN MYSELF SUCH ORDINARY FEMALE VANITY..
MARRY ME AND MAKE ME A BLUE-EYED BABY...
YOU'VE ALREADY WALKED OUT ON ONE FAMILY!!
AS A RULE, THE WORSE THE ORDEAL, THE COOLER I BECOME...
MAYBE IT'S TIME TO HANG IT UP MOMMY!

BESIDES, WHY WOULD I WANT TO GIVE UP STANDING IN UGLY DIRTY HALLS, FACING DULL PEOPLE WITH MY SOUL TURNED INSIDE OUT?!
YOU ARE SUCH A POWERFUL CREATURE, IT'S DIFFICULT TO BE A SIMPLE LOVER TO YOU...
HOT
CITY OF SAN DIEGO
THE FOLLOWING YEAR, BEN INSISTED ON RETURNING TO SAN DIEGO, HOPING TO CONQUER HIS FEARS...
NO PLAY WAS EVER STAGED WITH GREATER MELODRAMA THAN OUR ESCAPE FROM SAN DIEGO!!
EMMA MADE HER WAY BACK TO NEW YORK CITY ALONE... IN CHICAGO, SHE LEARNED OF THE DEATH OF VOLTAIRINE.
THE FUTILE PATERSON STRIKE AND THE MASSACRE OF THE LUDLOW MINERS MARKED THE DECLINE OF RADICAL LABOR. THE IWW WAS FORCED TO GIVE UP STREET ORGANIZING. MOTHER EARTH SANK INTO DEBT.
ALL SHE ASKED FOR WAS TO BE BURIED NEAR THE HAYMARKET MARTYRS, HER GRAVE DECKED WITH RED FLOWERS...
SHE LIVED AS THE POOREST OF THE POOR, SUSTAINED ONLY BY HER IDEAL, BEAUTIFUL IN HER SPIRITUAL DEFIANCE.
MOTHER EARTH
WE'LL HAVE TO CUT 12 LINES FROM THE WHEATFIELD STORY, STELLA...
EMMA MOVED TO SMALLER QUARTERS AND PUBLISHED HER COLLECTED ESSAYS TO PAY OFF THE BILLS... SASHA FINALLY LEFT TO START HIS OWN LABOR NEWSPAPER– THE BLAST.
BEN WAS NOT OF THE TEXTURE OF BERKMAN, WHO HAD COURAGE ENOUGH FOR A DOZEN MEN... BUT WHAT HE COULD GIVE, BEN GAVE WITHOUT RESTRAINT...
PRISON MEMOIRS of an ANARCHIST by A. BERKMAN
HIS BEST YEARS, HIS TREMENDOUS ZEST FOR WORK, HE DEVOTED TO ME...
FEW MEN HAVE DONE SO FOR A WOMAN.
©Sharon Rudahl '06

AS EARLY 20TH CENTURY WOMEN **LEFT HOME** TO STUDY AND WORK, THEY DEMANDED THE RIGHT TO POLITICAL REPRESENTATION. BY 1912, **NINE STATES** HAD GRANTED **2 MILLION** WOMEN THE **VOTE**. IN 1920, THE **19TH AMENDMENT** ADDED THIS RIGHT TO THE U.S. CONSTITUTION.

BUT **WOMAN SUFFRAGE** – EQUAL RIGHTS AT THE BALLOT BOX – WAS ONE PROGRESSIVE CAUSE EMMA **DID NOT** EMBRACE...

WOMAN SUFFRAGE
VOTES FOR WOMEN

BECAUSE SHE WAS AN **ANARCHIST**, EMMA DID NOT TRUST EVEN AN **ELECTED** CENTRAL GOVERNMENT.

SHE SCORNED SUFFRAGE AS A DEMAND OF COMFORTABLE, **MIDDLE CLASS** WOMEN...

WOMEN'S RIGHTS
VOTES FOR WOMEN
NATIONAL WOMAN'S PARTY

IN A **REPUBLIC** THERE ARE MANY WAYS FOR THE **STRONG**, THE **CUNNING**, AND THE **RICH** TO **SEIZE** POWER AND **HOLD IT**!!!

VOTES FOR WOMEN IS A **PARLOR** AFFAIR, ABSOLUTELY DETACHED FROM THE **ECONOMIC** NEEDS OF THE **PEOPLE**!

EMMA **REJECTED** THE ARGUMENT THAT WOMEN SHOULD VOTE BECAUSE THEY ARE **CLEANER**, MORE **CHASTE** AND **BETTER-BEHAVED** THAN MEN...

I AM NOT OPPOSED TO WOMAN SUFFRAGE ON THE CONVENTIONAL GROUND THAT SHE IS NOT **EQUAL** TO IT... BUT YOU SEE **YOUR** SLAVERY APART FROM THE HUMAN FAMILY.

VOTES FOR WOMEN

WOMEN NEED THE VOTE TO FULFILL THEIR **NATURAL** RESPONSIBILITIES– TO CURB **DRUNKENNESS** AND **PROSTITUTION**!

YOU'RE A **MAN'S WOMAN** AND **NOT ONE** OF **US**!!!

WOMAN **SUFFRAGE** WILL MEAN MORE **MEDDLING** AND REGULATING **MORALS**!

WHAT IS **GAINED** IF THE **NARROWNESS** OF THE **HOME** IS EXCHANGED FOR THE NARROWNESS OF THE **OFFICE** OR **FACTORY**?

TRUE LIBERATION BEGINS IN A WOMAN'S SOUL...

EMMA GAVE HER "NEW WOMAN" TALKS BEFORE ANYONE KNEW THERE WAS A NEW WOMAN. SHE SMOKED, DRANK AND LIVED OPENLY WITH HER LOVERS.
WHAT IS CONDEMNED AS VICE, SUCH AS MASTURBATION AND HOMOSEXUALITY...
...SHOULD NOT BE CONSIDERED IN A MORALIZING WAY!
IN THE YEARS JUST BEFORE WWI, EMMA WAS THE DARLING OF YOUNGER GREENWICH VILLAGE BOHEMIANS, INCLUDING WRITERS EUGENE O'NEILL, JACK REED, & LOUISE BRYANT, ARTISTS JOHN SLOAN AND ROBERT HENRI...
WASHINGTON SQUARE
CIGARS
CAFE
OASIS
FOR A WOMAN OF YOUR KNOWLEDGE, YOU ARE STRANGELY INNOCENT...
...MORE THAN ONCE, SHE ATTRACTED THE LOVE OF OTHER WOMEN...
EMMA'S YOUNG FANS WERE MORE INTERESTED IN MODERN THEATER THAN ECONOMIC THEORIES...
LAGE THEATRE
"GERMINAL" THE WELSH PLAY
The Social Significance of the Modern Drama by EMMA GOLDMA
"THE THEATER REFLECTS ALL LIFE... IT IS THE DYNAMITE THAT SHAKES THE SOCIAL PILLARS."
SHE WAS EVEN OFFERED A BOOKING ON OSCAR HAMMERSTEIN'S VAUDEVILLE STAGE!!
...TEN MINUTES BETWEEN THE TRAINED DOGS AND THE HIGH KICKERS!
BUT HOW MUCH WOULD THEY PAY?!
(AFTER THEIR OBSESSIVE AFFAIR ENDED, BEN REITMAN CONTINUED TO MANAGE EMMA'S SPEAKING CAREER...)
WITH EXPANDING CULTURAL FREEDOM, THE NEED FOR BIRTH CONTROL CAME OUT FROM THE SHADOWS. THIS ISSUE CUT ACROSS CLASS LINES... SINCE HER DAYS AS A MIDWIFE, EMMA HAD BEEN A PASSIONATE ADVOCATE FOR CONTRACEPTION.
Speaker: 8 P.M. "THE FAILURE OF CHRISTIANITY" EMMA GOLDMAN
PURITANISM FORCES THE WOMAN TO BEAR CHILDREN IN SPITE OF WEAKENED PHYSICAL CONDITION OR ECONOMIC INABILITY.
THE 1873 COMSTOCK ACT CRIMINALIZED BIRTH CONTROL DEVICES AND INFORMATION. IN THE LATE 1800S, A FEW BRAVE SOULS SPOKE OUT AND SUFFERED ARREST AND RUIN. FOR YEARS, EMMA SKIRTED THE EDGE OF THE COMSTOCK LAWS...
FREEDOM IN LOVE FREEDOM IN MOTHERHOOD
A WOMAN MUST BE FREE TO DECIDE THE NUMBER OF CHILDREN SHE IS TO BRING INTO THE WORLD!
©Sharon Rudahl '06

THE GREAT U.S. PIONEER OF BIRTH CONTROL WAS MARGARET SANGER, A SOCIAL ACTIVIST NURSE. HER BIRTH CONTROL LEAGUE EVOLVED INTO PLANNED PARENTHOOD...
YOU'LL FIND WHAT YOU'RE LOOKING FOR IN HERE.
The WOMAN REBEL
MARGARET SANGER
1883-1966
"TO CHANGE THE DESTINY OF MOTHERS WHOSE MISERIES WERE AS VAST AS THE SKY."
IN 1914, AN ENTIRE ISSUE OF THE WOMAN REBEL WAS CONFISCATED BY THE POST OFFICE. SANGER'S HUSBAND WILLIAM WAS ARRESTED FOR GIVING A BIRTH CONTROL PAMPHLET TO A COP.
I MUST STOP LECTURING ABOUT CONTRACEPTION — OR DO IT PRACTICAL JUSTICE!
YOUR BIRTH CONTROL TALKS ALWAYS SELL THE MOST TICKETS!
SANGER ARREST BOOKS SEIZED
EMMA GAVE EXPLICIT INSTRUCTIONS TO PREVENT PREGNANCY, WHILE BEN DISTRIBUTED CONDOMS AND DIAPHRAGMS TO SELL-OUT CROWDS. THEY TOURED A DOZEN CITIES SAFELY...
YER UNDER ARREST!
WE'RE CONFISCATING THAT FILTH!!
...BUT ON FEBRUARY 11, 1916, THEY GOT BUSTED IN NEW YORK CITY...
AT HER TRIAL, EMMA SPOKE FOR AN HOUR IN HER OWN DEFENSE.
LARGE FAMILIES ARE A MILLSTONE AROUND THE NECKS OF WORKING PEOPLE!
...TO CONDEMN WOMAN TO CONTINUAL CHILD-BEARING MAKES HER THE ENEMY OF MAN!
IF IT IS A CRIME TO WORK FOR HEALTHY MOTHERHOOD, FOR JOYOUS CHILDHOOD, FOR THE BETTERMENT OF THE HUMAN RACE — YOUR HONOUR, I AM GLAD AND PROUD TO BE A CRIMINAL!
CLCLAP
HURRAH!!
CLAP CLAP CLAP CLAP
WHEN EMMA FINISHED SPEAKING, THE ENTIRE COURTROOM BURST INTO APPLAUSE!
EMMA CHOSE 15 DAYS IN THE QUEENS WORKHOUSE INSTEAD OF A FINE. BEN SERVED 60 DAYS IN QUEENS, AND 6 MONTHS IN CLEVELAND... AS EMMA TURNED FROM THE BIRTH CONTROL CAMPAIGN TO CONFRONT THE DRUMS OF WAR, DR. REITMAN FOUGHT ON FOR CONTRACEPTION AS A PUBLIC HEALTH ISSUE.
WE WERE NOT THE PIONEERS OF THE BIRTH CONTROL MOVEMENT, BUT WE POPULARIZED THE QUESTION...
...EMMA GOLDMAN WAS THE FIRST AND LAST TO GIVE ACTUAL METHODS FROM THE PLATFORM.
© Sharon Rudahl '06

AS THE FLAMES OF WORLD WAR I SPREAD ACROSS EUROPE, HELENA PROUDLY INVITED EMMA TO HER SON DAVID'S FIRST SOLO VIOLIN CONCERT, PERFORMING WITH THE ROCHESTER SYMPHONY...
BRILLIANT!
BRAVO!!
GERMAN EMPIRE
POLAND
AUSTRO-HUNGARIAN EMPIRE
BELGIUM
SWITZERLAND
SERVIA
FRANCE
ITALY
SO WHAT DO YOU THINK OF YOUR LITTLE COUSIN NOW, STELLA?!
DAVID IS TRULY A FINISHED ARTIST!
ALL HELENA'S FIERCE LOVE, HER SACRIFICES AND HUMBLE HOPES ARE NOW FULFILLED...
THE U.S. SEETHED WITH JINGOIST HYSTERIA. WOODROW WILSON WON REELECTION ON A PROMISE TO "KEEP US OUT OF WAR". BUT THE POWER BROKERS CRAVED THEIR SHARE OF POST-WAR REPARATIONS AND AUTHORITY
PREPAREDNESS~THE ROAD TO UNIVERSAL SLAUGHTER
NO WAR
MOTHER EARTH
INTERNATIONAL ANARCHIST MANIFESTO
WE OPPOSE THIS STATE WAR BUT SUPPORT THE ONE WAR OF LIBERATION BY THE OPPRESSED
AFTER HER STINT IN THE WORKHOUSE FOR DISTRIBUTING BIRTH CONTROL, EMMA WENT ON TOUR URGING RESISTANCE TO THE WAR...
"PREPAREDNESS" HAS AT ALL TIMES AND IN ALL COUNTRIES PRECIPITATED ARMED CONFLICT!!
THIS CAPITALIST WAR IS BEING FOUGHT TO ENRICH THE PRIVILEGED FEW AND HELP THEM TO SUBDUE LABOR!!
JULY 1916
SASHA'S LABOR PAPER THE BLAST WAS PUBLISHED IN SAN FRANCISCO. EMMA CAME TO CALIFORNIA TO GIVE HER LECTURES "THE SPECULATORS IN WAR AND STARVATION." AT THE INDEPENDENCE DAY PREPAREDNESS PARADE, A BOMB EXPLODED.
READ ALL ABOUT IT! ANARCHIST BOMB!!
SAN FRANCISCO EXAMINER
TEN KILLED
ANARCHIST ATTACK
FREE TOM MOONEY
The Blast
FREE TOM MOONEY
The Blast
THE WORKERS, THEY ALONE CAN AVERT THE IMPENDING WAR, IN FACT ALL WARS IF THEY WILL REFUSE TO BE A PARTY TO THEM!
LABOR ORGANIZER TOM MOONEY WAS FRAMED FOR THE BOMBING. THE PROSECUTOR TRIED TO CONNECT SASHA AND EMMA.
© Sharon Rudahl '06

ON APRIL 6, 1917 THE U.S. ENTERED WORLD WAR I – "TO MAKE THE WORLD SAFE FOR DEMOCRACY." AS CONGRESS DEBATED THE SELECTIVE SERVICE ACT, EMMA AND SASHA RETURNED TO NEW YORK TO START AN ANTI-DRAFT LEAGUE
LUSITANIA SUNK BY HUN
WE CAN RENT THE HARLEM RIVER CASINO FOR OUR FIRST MASS MEETING!!
TEN THOUSAND PEOPLE PACKED THE FIRST "ANTI-CONSCRIPTION LEAGUE" MEETING... TO DODGE LAWS AGAINST INTERFERING WITH THE DRAFT, THEY SUPPORTED CONSCIENTIOUS OBJECTION...
NEXT MEETING JUNE 4!
JOIN US!!
PEACE NOW
FREE BORN AMERICANS ARE TO BE FORCIBLY IMPRESSED INTO THE MILITARY, HERDED LIKE CATTLE, AND SHIPPED OFF TO FERTILIZE THE FIELDS OF FRANCE!!!
AT THE JUNE 4 MEETING, THUGS IN UNIFORM UNSCREWED THE LIGHT-BULBS AND THREW THEM AT THE SPEAKERS –
SPIES!
TRAITORS!!
HUNS!
YOU'RE ALL UNDER ARREST!
PLEASE, LET'S ALL FILE OUT SINGING THE INTERNATIONALE!
"ARISE, YE PRISONERS OF STARVATION, ARISE, YE WRETCHED OF THE EARTH..."
FRIENDS, WE'RE HERE BECAUSE WE DO NOT BELIEVE IN SENSELESS VIOLENCE!! WE MUST REFUSE TO BE PROVOKED!
EMMA'S COOLNESS NARROWLY AVERTED A RIOT
AT THE THIRD AND LAST ANTI-CONSCRIPTION MEETING, EMMA'S NIECE STELLA BALLANTINE TOOK THE PLATFORM FOR THE FIRST TIME...
PEACE NOW
AS YOU SEE, I'VE BECOME A MOTHER...
... LIKE EVERY MOTHER, MY BABY'S LIFE IS EVERYTHING TO ME...
HOW CAN WE MOTHERS LET OUR CHILDREN'S BLOOD BE SPILLED TO ENRICH THE WAR PROFITEERS??
LEAVING THE HALL, EVERY MAN WHO COULD NOT PRODUCE A DRAFT CARD WAS ARRESTED
©Sharon Rudahl 06

THE NEXT DAY, POLICE RANSACKED THE MOTHER EARTH OFFICE AND TOOK EMMA AND SASHA INTO CUSTODY.
FOREIGN STUFF!
LOOKS LIKE TREASON TO ME!
WAR AND PEACE BY LEO TOLSTOY
POEMS OF FRIEDRICH SCHILLER
FAUST JOHANN GOETHE
SUPPORTERS RAISED THE $50,000 BAIL. EMMA AND SASHA INSISTED ON ARGUING THEIR OWN CASE. JOHN REED, LINCOLN STEFFENS AND OTHER NOTABLES TESTIFIED IN THEIR DEFENSE.
STENOGRAPHIC EVIDENCE PROVES THE ACCUSED URGE VIOLENCE AGAINST THE STATE!
WE ONLY SUPPORT CONSCIENTIOUS OBJECTION—
SILENCE OR I'LL CHARGE YOU WITH CONTEMPT!!
EVERY ONE OF YOU IS A PEACEFUL, LAW-ABIDING CITIZEN, YET YOU SUPPORT THIS MURDEROUS WAR!
IF AMERICA ENTERED THIS WAR TO MAKE THE WORLD SAFE FOR DEMOCRACY, SHE MUST FIRST MAKE DEMOCRACY SAFE IN AMERICA!
FIRST NAT BANK
PAY to the Order of $3,000.
YOUR HONOR, THIS $3,000 CHECK WAS DEPOSITED TWO DAYS BEFORE THEIR ARREST – PROVING THE ACCUSED ARE IN THE PAY OF THE HUN!!!
HONORABLE SIR, THAT IS MY CHECK, SIR... MY LIFE SAVINGS... MISS GOLDMAN IS DOING WORK I BELIEVE IN...
THE JURY TOOK 39 MINUTES TO CONVICT—
WHAMP!
WE HAVE NO PLACE IN THIS COUNTRY FOR THOSE WHO EXPRESS THE VIEW THE LAW MAY BE DISOBEYED!
$10,000 FINE, TWO YEARS IMPRISONMENT... THIS COURT RECOMMENDS THAT YOU THEN BE REMANDED FOR DEPORTATION—
© Sharon Rudahl '06

WARTIME AMERICA UNITED TO PERSECUTE LABOR ORGANIZERS, STIFLE DISSENT AND HARASS IMMIGRANTS...
PROGRESSIVE SCHOOLS WERE SHUT DOWN. VIGILANTES BROKE UP UNION MEETINGS. MASS TRIALS CRUSHED THE IWW. SOCIALIST EUGENE V. DEBS HAD WON 6% OF THE POPULAR VOTE FOR PRESIDENT IN 1912. HE BELATEDLY SPOKE OUT AGAINST THE ROUT OF CIVIL LIBERTIES...
100 PERCENT PATRIOTS
BOOKS
BOUGHT & SOLD
UNITED WE STAND
HEINRICH HEINE POEMS
YOU'RE BREAKING THE LAW, BUDDY - SELLING THIS ENEMY TRASH!
by Thomas Mann
VIOLATION OF THE 1917 ESPIONAGE ACT— DISLOYAL LANGUAGE ABOUT THE GOVERNMENT OR FLAG – MR. DEBS, THIS COURT SENTENCES YOU TO TEN YEARS!!
EMMA HAD SIX MONTHS AT LIBERTY, WHILE HER LAWYER HARRY WEINBERGER APPEALED TO THE SUPREME COURT.
FORBIDDEN BY THE TERMS OF HER RELEASE TO SPEAK IN SASHA'S DEFENSE, EMMA APPEARED ON STAGE GAGGED...
ANTI-WAR NEWS!
MORE CONTRIBUTIONS!! COULDN'T WE TRY BAILING SASHA OUT OF THE TOMBS?
FREE ALEXA BERKMA
PEAC NOW!
SUPPORT MEETING FOR ALEXANDER BERKMAN!
NO, STELLA, HE'S SAFER THERE. IF HE'S KIDNAPPED BACK TO CALIFORNIA, THEY'LL HANG HIM WITH MOONEY FOR THE 4TH OF JULY BOMBING.
REPEATED POLICE RAIDS SHUT DOWN MOTHER EARTH, BUT EMMA AND STELLA MANAGED TO PRINT AND DISTRIBUTE 8 PAGE MOTHER EARTH BULLETINS.
ONCE MORE EXPELLED BY A FEARFUL LANDLORD, EMMA TOOK REFUGE WITH HER RECENTLY WIDOWED SISTER HELENA.
SURPRISED, AUNT EMMA?! I WAIVED EXEMPTION AND VOLUNTEERED!
DAVID REFUSED TO TELL THE DOCTORS ABOUT HIS WEAK LUNGS...
HELENA WILL NOT SURVIVE THE VAIN SACRIFICE OF HER SON...
EMMA WORKED AGAINST THE CLOCK TO EXPOSE PERJURED TESTIMONY IN THE MOONEY CASE AND SAVE SASHA FROM EXTRADITION —
REFUGEES FROM NEW YORK DELIVERED OUR MESSAGE — DEMONSTRATIONS FOR SASHA IN PETROGRAD AND KRONSTADT!!
THE JEWISH ANARCHISTS ARE HOLDING A RALLY!
© Sharon Rudahl '06

AT KRONSTADT ARMED RUSSIAN SAILORS HELD THE U.S. AMBASSADOR HOSTAGE, DEMANDING PRESIDENT WILSON INTERVENE TO SAVE SASHA.
WASHINGTON LEANED ON SAN FRANCISCO—THEY WON'T PRESS FOR BERKMAN'S EXTRADITION...
TAKE YER FELLA AWAY FOR THE LOVE OF MIKE!!
RELEASED ON BAIL, SASHA & EMMA POURED OUT THEIR REMAINING LIBERTY AT MASS ANTI-WAR MEETINGS ACROSS THE MIDWEST...
I'D LIKE TO READ A MESSAGE FROM A REMARKABLE COMRADE—
MY VERY HEART IS IN THE STRUGGLE THAT IS TO INAUGURATE A FREER, HAPPIER SOCIETY. YOU CAN COUNT ON MY LOVE AND SUPPORT. NEVER WERE COURAGE AND FORTITUDE SO NEEDED AS NOW. Helen Keller transcribed by Anne Sullivan
HELEN KELLER 1880~1968
OCTOBER
A RENT IN THE DARKNESS—THE BOLSHEVIK REVOLUTION OF 1917! EMMA HAD LONG CRITICIZED THE MARXIST IDEAL OF A WORKERS' DICTATORSHIP—BUT WITH MANY MILLIONS WHO OPPOSED WAR AND INJUSTICE, SHE WAS SWEPT UP IN A TIDE OF HOPE.
THE DAY SO LONG YEARNED FOR HAD ARRIVED AT LAST!
Lecture: The Bolsheviki REVOLUTION ITS PROMISE AND Fulfillme
IN ONE MIGHTY VOICE, THE PEOPLE OF RUSSIA THUNDERED FOR PEACE, FOR BROTHERHOOD WITH THE PEOPLE OF GERMANY AND ALL THE DISINHERITED AND OPPRESSED!!!
EMMA'S PACIFIST LAWYER LOST HIS APPEAL TO THE SUPREME COURT. FOUR MONTHS AFTER THE RUSSIAN REVOLUTION, EMMA AND SASHA WERE ORDERED TO SURRENDER TO FEDERAL AUTHORITIES.
...HEAR TELL SHE'S A GERMAN SPY!
NAH, SHE'S A BOLSHEVIK AGENT.
TWO YEARS IMPRISONMENT FOR AN UNCOMPROMISING STAND FOR ONE'S IDEAL—WHY, THAT IS A SMALL PRICE...
THE MISSOURI STATE PRISON HOUSED 100 WOMEN, IN MORE MODERN CELLS THAN AT BLACKWELL'S ISLAND. BUT THEY DID FORCED LABOR NINE HOURS A DAY IN A DANK SWEATSHOP...
MEET YOUR QUOTA TODAY, ERLENE, OR IT'S THE BLIND CELL!
I FOUND NO CRIMINALS, ONLY UNFORTUNATES—BROKEN, HAPLESS AND HELPLESS HUMAN BEINGS...
© Sharon Rudahl '06

UNRULY WOMEN WERE FLOGGED OR STARVED. EMMA'S HEALTH BROKE DOWN. BUT INFLUENTIAL FRIENDS CONVINCED THE PRISON OFFICIALS TO LOOK AFTER THEIR STAR BOARDER...
A CELL WITH A VIEW!!
WARDEN SAYS YOU CAN KEEP THE MATTRESS YOUR PALS SENT- AND A BIG PACKET OF BOOKS, SOON AS HE'S LOOKED 'EM OVER.
EMMA RE-COVERED THE DAMP, BLOTCHED WALLS OF HER CELL WITH CRÊPE-PAPER.
"PRISON LIFE TENDS TO MAKE ONE WONDROUSLY RESOURCEFUL"
HAD WE MET ON THE OUTSIDE WE WOULD HAVE ARGUED FURIOUSLY AND REMAINED STRANGERS-
BUT YOU REALLY SHOULDN'T TEASE ME SO ABOUT THE TIME I SPEND CURLING MY HAIR!
EMMA FORMED A SISTERHOOD WITH SOCIALIST KATE O'HARE, SENTENCED TO 5 YEARS FOR AN ANTI-WAR SPEECH, AND GABRIELA ANTOLINI, A YOUNG ANTI-WAR ANARCHIST...
AS AT BLACKWELL'S ISLAND, EMMA SHARED EVERYTHING SHE RECEIVED WITH OTHER PRISONERS.
"EMMA DID THINGS FOR THEM. SHE FOUGHT FOR THEM WHEN THEY WERE WRONGED, SHE FED THEM WHEN THEY WERE HUNGRY, AND CARED FOR THEM WHEN THEY WERE ILL. THE WOMEN WORSHIPPED HER"
WE ARE SERVED ONLY COLD, STALE FOOD...
FRESH HOT STEW IN THE DINING HALL, GIRLS!
... THE SICK AND THE HEALTHY SHARE THE SAME STAGNANT BATH WATER...
KATE CAME FROM A HIGH-CLASS FAMILY. HER HUSBAND PUBLISHED THE POPULAR NATIONAL RIPSAW. WHEN SHE COMPLAINED, SHE GOT RESULTS.
COME SEE!! THEY'RE PUTTING IN REAL SHOWER BATHS!!
ON CHRISTMAS EVE, WHILE THE OTHER WOMEN WERE AT CHURCH SERVICES, EMMA AND KATE GOT PERMISSION TO PLAY SANTA WITH DONATED TREASURES...
ROSE-WATER SOAP!!
PRALINE CANDY! FACE CREAM!!
LIPSTICK!
STOCKINGS!
GLOVES! RIBBONS!
A LACE HANKY!!
STRAWBERRY JAM!
A PINK WOOL BLANKET!
EMMA WAS NOTORIOUS FOR HER CRAMPED HANDWRITING AND SLOPPY TYPING. KATE DEMANDED A TYPEWRITER AND TOOK ON THE ROLE OF SECRETARY...
...CORRECT GALLEYS OF MANIFESTO... FUND-RAISING FOR SASHA'S DEFENSE... TO JOHN REED—CONGRATULATIONS ON SUCCESS OF TEN DAYS THAT SHOOK THE WORLD...
LETTER TO THE...
SCHEDULE...
...RALLY...
BAIL...
LEAFLET...

EMMA SPENT HER 50TH BIRTHDAY IN PRISON, DELUGED WITH CARDS AND GIFTS FROM ALL OVER. COMRADE BILL SHATOFF SENT ROSES FROM RUSSIA. HER FIRST CLOSE AFRICAN-AMERICAN FRIENDS PREPARED A SPECIAL TREAT.
THAT LOOKS LIKE A FULL DAY'S QUOTA!
WE THOUGHT IT WOULD BE SO NICE IF MISS EMMA COULD KEEP OUT OF THE SHOP ON HER BIRTHDAY...
Happy Birthday
BUT AMONG THE CHEERFUL GREETINGS WAS ONE PIECE OF TRAGIC NEWS...
WHAT IS IT EMMA?!
MY SISTER GOT CONFIRMATION FROM THE WAR OFFICE- HER SON DAVID DIED IN THE ARGONNE FOREST A MONTH BEFORE THE ARMISTICE.
EXILE TO EXILE
THE END OF WORLD WAR I ONLY INTENSIFIED ATTACKS ON DISSIDENTS, NOW BRANDED "REDS" INSTEAD OF GERMAN SPIES. AMBITIOUS YOUNG J. EDGAR HOOVER LED RAIDS FOR HIS BOSS PALMER, AND WAS PUT IN CHARGE OF A NEW RADICAL DIVISION IN THE U.S. JUSTICE DEPT. U.S.-BORN POLITICAL PRISONERS WERE GIVEN DECADES-LONG SENTENCES. EMMA WAS ONE OF HUNDREDS OF IMMIGRANTS SUMMARILY DEPORTED...
...SASHA'S CASE IS HOPELESS, HE NEVER WAS A CITIZEN. BUT WEINBERGER WILL CONTEST THE SHADY WAY THEY CANCELLED YOUR CITIZENSHIP AFTER KERSNER DIED—
STELLA, DID I TELL YOU HARRY KELLY OFFERED TO GET MARRIED?!?
OLD SAM SICKLES WANTS TO ADOPT YOU!
ON SEPTEMBER 27, 1919, EMMA LEFT THE MISSOURI STATE PRISON, WITH A FEW MONTHS AT LIBERTY BEFORE HER DEPORTATION HEARING.
BUT EMMA DRIFTED WITH HER LAWYER'S STRATEGY INSTEAD OF PUTTING UP HER USUAL FIGHT...
SASHA HAD BEEN MY COMRADE, FRIEND AND CO-WORKER THROUGH THIRTY YEARS... IT WAS UNTHINKABLE THAT HE SHOULD JOIN THE REVOLUTION AND I REMAIN BEHIND...

On her way home to N.Y.C., Emma met with Dr. Ben Reitman and his new WIFE and CHILD
She visited her mother and sisters in Rochester...
Helena had become a LIFELESS, BENT OLD WOMAN... since David's death, her life was ebbing out in TEARS...
Taube invited Emma to "speak a piece" at the opening of her PET PROJECT - a Jewish orphanage and home for the aged.
Your REVOLUTION is all very good for the FUTURE, daughter, but what is to become of our widows and orphans NOW?!
Weakened by illness caused by harsh prison conditions, Sasha joined Emma on their LAST U.S. speaking tour...
I deny the right of anyone to set up an inquisition of THOUGHT!!
Always they were dogged by the Justice Department. One agent, Margaret Scully, offered her services as a stenographer-
After two weeks, Emma fired her for SHOWING UP LATE-
As I am fond of Goldie and SORRY for Sasha, it is well I am no longer forced to DECEIVE our comrades.
The press fueled hysteria against Russian immigrants -
RED BOMB LAB DISCOVERED
ATTORNEY GENERAL LISTS 60,000 REDS
PATRIOTS BURN BOLSHI BOOKS
KU KLUX KLAN PLANS MARCH
RED PROFESSOR EXPOSED BY TOP STUDENT
Emma still had FAITHFUL supporters... heiress Aline Barnsdall rushed from California to deliver a $5,000 check...
I INSIST - for your expenses abroad...
...to be DRIVEN OUT of the land I called my own ALL my adult life is NOT a cheerful prospect - but what I dreaded MOST was financial DEPENDENCE...
Your check will keep me FREE!
© Sharon Rudahl '06

December 2 1919 – Reporters dashed into the farewell dinner presented by Chicago comrades
Mr. Berkman – Henry Clay Frick just suffered a fatal heart attack – do you have any comment for the press?
Press
Deported by God!!
Dec. 8 – Emma and Sasha ordered to appear at immigration court on Ellis Island. Judge Julius Mayer quickly rejected all of lawyer Weinberger's arguments...
Don't give up fighting, sailor girl...
Rather than give our enemies another chance to defeat me, I have decided to tell them all to go to hell!
Emma shared her Ellis Island cell with Dora Lipkin and Ethel Bernstein...
We weren't accused of any crime... the cops just said they were sending us back to Russia –
But we don't know anybody in Russia!!
Each day, "Red Special" trains discharged more bewildered, penniless deportees... with Stella's help, Emma raised donations of warm clothes, canned food, and medical supplies... with Sasha she composed and smuggled out a 32 page tract.
Deportation – its meaning and significance
Emma Goldm
Alexander Be
Emma wrote her last instructions and farewells, this to Dr. Ben Reitman:
Dearest Hobo, Their mad rush in getting us out of the country is the greatest proof that I have served the cause of humanity.
Love, Emma
©Sharon Rudahl '06
December 21 1919 – In the dead of night, the prisoners were shouted awake –
March!!
Line up!
Emma carried a typewriter, others banjos and guitars...
Arise ye prisoners of starvation...
Arise, ye wretched of the earth...

3 AM— THE DEPORTEES MARCHED THRU FREEZING SNOW BETWEEN LINES OF HEAVILY ARMED SOLDIERS.
AMERICA, THE LAND OF FREEDOM, REPEATING THE TERRIBLE SCENES OF TSARIST RUSSIA...
EMMA, SASHA AND 248 OTHERS WERE HERDED ABOARD THE DECREPIT ARMY TRANSPORT BUFORD-
AT 6 A.M., THEY GOT THEIR LAST LOOK AT THE STATUE OF LIBERTY.
THE BUFORD WAS A LEAKY SCOW, WITH ONLY 2 TOILETS FOR THE MEN CROWDED BELOW DECKS... BUT THEY SET TO WORK ORGANIZING THE CREW...
YOU LOST FRIENDS IN THE WAR, RIGHT? YOU WENT THROUGH HELL. BUT WHEN YOU CAME BACK, THE RICH MEN'S SONS WERE RUNNING EVERYTHING...
WE COULD SEIZE ARMS, TIE UP THE OFFICERS, AND JOIN YOU!
WE'VE PUT YOUR MEN IN THE BAKERY, THAT SHOULD IMPROVE THE FOOD SITUATION-
AFTER PASSING THROUGH THE MINE STREWN ENGLISH CHANNEL, THE BUFORD HAD TO PUT IN FOR REPAIRS AT HAMBURG, GERMANY.
BUFORD
THREE CHEERS FOR DIE SOZIALE REVOLUTION!!!
HURRAH!!
HURRAH!!
HURRAH!!!
ON JANUARY 16 1920, THE DEPORTEES LANDED AT HANGO, FINLAND...
HER FEVER IS WORSE!
I TRIED TO GET A TIN OF BROTH, BUT THE GUARDS STOLE EVERYTHING-
AN UNHEATED TRAIN MANNED BY ANTI-RED FINNISH SOLDIERS CARTED THEM TOWARD THE RUSSIAN BORDER...
RUSSIA THERE!
YOU, WALK! GET GOING!!
©Sharon Rudahl '06

THE BUFORD DEPORTEES WERE AFRAID RUSSIAN BORDER GUARDS WOULD SHOOT THEM DOWN AS INVADING FINNS.
GIVE ME A FINNISH OFFICER AS ESCORT, AND I'LL GO ACROSS.
AS SASHA REACHED THE FROZEN CREEK MARKING THE BORDER, HEAVY SNOWFALL OBSCURED HIS VIEW-
HULOOOO! TOVARICH!! HALOOOOOOOO!
COMRADES!
AT LAST!!
THERE'S A WELCOMING COMMITTEE WAITING FOR YOU!
SLEIGHS TRANSPORTED THE DEPORTEES ACROSS THE ICE, WHILE A *SOVIET MILITARY BAND PLAYED THE INTERNATIONALE
AT LAST WE WERE ON THE THRESHOLD OF REVOLUTIONARY RUSSIA! MY HEART TREMBLED WITH FERVENT HOPE...
LAND! BREAD! AN END TO SENSELESS WAR!
* SOVIET~ A DIRECTLY ELECTED COUNCIL REPRESENTING COMMON WORKERS, SOLDIERS AND PEASANTS. LOCAL COUNCILS VOTED FOR AREA COUNCILS, A HIERARCHY HEADED BY THE SUPREME SOVIET.
Welcome to
LENINGRAD
St. Petersburg
PETERSBURG
WHEN EMMA AND SASHA ARRIVED IN THE CITY THEY HAD KNOWN AS ST. PETERSBURG, THEY WERE HOUSED IN THE ELEGANT HOTEL ASTORIA, ALONGSIDE HIGH-RANKING OFFICIALS..
THE HOUSES LIKE BROKEN OLD TOMBS, THE STREETS DESERTED, THE PEOPLE LIVING CORPSES... THE SHORTAGE OF FOOD AND FUEL WAS SLOWLY SAPPING THE CITY.
© Sharon Rudahl '06
WHY AREN'T CREWS ORGANIZED TO CUT FIREWOOD?? WHY ARE THERE 34 GRADES OF RATIONS?
THE REVOLUTION IS FIGHTING FOR ITS LIFE AGAINST WHITE ARMIES AND THE INVADING ALLIES!! MEDICINES AND FOOD IMPORTS ARE CUT OFF BY BLOCKADE—
FAMOUS JOURNALIST JOHN REED DASHED BY TO WELCOME EMMA-

THOUGH EMMA WAS THRILLED BY REVOLUTIONARY ART AND THEATER, HER MISGIVINGS DEEPENED...
SHE QUESTIONED HER HEROINES ALEXANDRA KOLLONTAI AND ANGELICA BALABANOFF...
WHY CLOSE THE UNIVERSITIES? WHY SO MUCH SABOTAGE AND WASTE?
THE REVOLUTION IS FIGHTING FOR ITS LIFE —
— AGAINST WHITE ARMIES AND THE ALLIED INVASION...
SHE SOUGHT OUT LEGENDARY VOICE OF THE PEOPLE MAXIM GORKY.
WHY MASS EXECUTIONS OF COUNTER-REVOLUTIONARIES?? WHY SECRET POLICE??? WHY WHOLESALE ARRESTS OF ANARCHISTS?
THE REVOLUTION IS FIGHTING FOR ITS LIFE...
GENTLE OLD PETER KROPOTKIN RETURNED FROM PARIS EXILE TO DESTITUTE ISOLATION...
SINCE WHEN DO REVOLUTIONARIES COLD-BLOODEDLY STAND PEOPLE AGAINST THE WALL?!
THE REVOLUTION IS FIGHTING FOR ITS LIFE - WOMEN AND CHILDREN ARE DYING FROM THE BLOCKADE.
WHEN I CONSIDER THE SAME MONSTER IS BEING SET UP IN RUSSIA, I GROW COLD ALL OVER.
A LIMO RUSHED SASHA AND EMMA TO A SECRET MEETING—
COMRADE LENIN ADMIRES YOU DEFY U.S. GOVERNMENT...
WE ANARCHISTS ALWAYS POINTED OUT THE DANGERS OF MARXISM IN ACTION— WHY BE SURPRISED NOW?
© Sharon Rudahl '07
THE TRIUMPH OF THE STATE MEANS THE DEFEAT OF THE REVOLUTION!
EMMA COULD NOT WORK AS A NURSE WITHOUT PLEDGING LOYALTY TO THE COMMUNIST PARTY. SHE AND SASHA TOOK AN ASSIGNMENT RESTORING VILLAS AS WORKERS' REST HOMES.
IT'S NO GOOD- I CAN'T EVICT ANYBODY - THEY'RE JUST TERRIFIED TEACHERS AND OFFICE CLERKS!
FREE SPEECH IS A BOURGEOIS PREJUDICE—FIND SOMETHING USEFUL TO DO.
DEAREST STELLA, I CANNOT TELL YOU HOW TORN AWAY I FEEL FROM ALL THAT WAS PRECIOUS TO ME... THE HIDEOUS SORES ON LENIN'S REVOLUTIONARY RUSSIA CANNOT BE IGNORED.
Dear Emma,
Death was kind and came gently to Helena.
Yours, Stella
Dearest Stella
LONG LIVE THE THIRD COMMUNIST INTERNATIONAL!
VIVE LA TROISIEME INTERNATIONALE COMMUNISTE!
VIVA IL TERZA INTERNAZIONALE COMMUNISTA!
ES LEBE DIE DRITTE KOMMUNISTISCHE INTERNATIONALE!
ВИНТОВКА-РЯДОМ

AFTER 4 MONTHS STATE BUREAUCRATS PUT EMMA AND SASHA IN CHARGE OF AN EXPEDITION FOR THE MUSEUM OF THE REVOLUTION.
WE'VE BEEN ASSIGNED A SECRETARY AND 2 DOCUMENTS EXPERTS- THAT LEFT WING REPORTER HARRY ALSBERG WANTS TO TAG ALONG...
SUPPLIES FROM THE WINTER PALACE BASEMENT- WE'LL BE EATING OUR CABBAGE OFF MATCHING CHINA WITH THE CZAR'S CREST!
THEY TRAVELED IN A PRIVATE PULLMAN CAR WITH 6 COMPARTMENTS, GATHERING REVOLUTIONARY PAPERS, PHOTOS, STAMPS, POSTERS AND BANNERS.
BROKEN CARS, DISABLED ENGINES, TORN-UP TRACK... AT EVERY STATION, EXHAUSTED PEOPLE FALLING OVER EACH OTHER TO SCRAMBLE ON...
THE MUSEUM TRAIN CROSSED THE UKRAINE, SWEPT BY THE RED ARMY, PETLURA & DENIKIN'S WHITE ARMIES AND NESTOR MAKNO'S FREE PEASANT MILITIA.
AT THE RUINS OF THE JEWISH VILLAGE FASTOV-
OVER 4,000 OF OUR PEOPLE PERISHED IN THE LAST MASSACRE-
OUR WIVES AND DAUGHTERS RAPED, THE OLD MEN TORTURED IN THE SYNAGOGUE..
WE BLESS LENIN FOR PUTTING AN END TO THE POGROMS!
... I DON'T KNOW HIS ADDRESS, BUT COULD YOU PLEASE TAKE THIS LETTER TO MY NEPHEW IN BROOKLYN?
... BROTHER? IN CHICAGO!
... COUSIN IN BALTIMORE?
ONE MOONLESS NIGHT, MAKNO'S WIFE GALINA APPEARED-
JOIN US FIGHTING THE BOLSHEVIKS! WE HAVE GIVEN THE PEASANTS SELF-DETERMINATION, FREE SCHOOLS, CLINICS, LAND—
THERE'S BEEN ENOUGH BLOOD SPILLED... JUST MEETING YOU PUTS EVERYONE ON THIS EXPEDITION IN MORTAL DANGER!!
WHAT CAN YOU EXPECT?! PEOPLE ARE DESPERATE...
BUT ALL WE HAD LEFT OF THE BARNSDALL MONEY WAS SEWN INTO THE LINING!!
AT A STATION BETWEEN ODESSA AND MOSCOW SASHA'S OVERCOAT WAS STOLEN—
© Sharon Rudahl '07

JOHN REED DIED OF TYPHUS AFTER BEING SENT ON A FUTILE MISSION TO BAKU. HE WAS THE FIRST AMERICAN BURIED IN RED SQUARE.
A GREY, DREARY DAY... NO BEAUTY FOR THE MAN WHO LOVED IT SO...
A MONTH LATER- FEBRUARY 1921- PETER KROPOTKIN DIED, HAILED AS A SOVIET HERO THOUGH HIS LAST MONTHS PASSED UNDER VIRTUAL HOUSE ARREST...
IF YOU DON'T LET PETER'S COMRADES OUT TO CARRY HIS COFFIN, I SWEAR THE WORLD PRESS WILL HAVE A FIELD DAY!
THAT WINTER WAS BITTERLY COLD. WHOLE LIBRARIES WERE BURNT FOR FUEL... CHOLERA, TYPHOID AND TYPHUS RAGED. THE KRONSTADT SAILORS, VANGUARD OF THE OCTOBER REVOLUTION, JOINED WORKERS STRIKING FOR BETTER RATIONS AND WARM CLOTHING... EMMA, SASHA AND THE OTHER BUFORD DEPORTEES OFFERED TO NEGOTIATE "A FRATERNAL REVOLUTIONARY AGREEMENT"...
THE ASSAULT ON KRONSTADT LASTED 11 DAYS. SIX HUNDRED SAILORS DIED, 1000'S WERE LATER SHOT OR EXILED. SASHA COULD HEAR THE BOMBARDMENT FROM HIS HOTEL ROOM...
MY HEART IS NUMB WITH DESPAIR ...SOMETHING HAS DIED WITHIN ME...
KROPOTKIN'S WIDOW SOPHIE PLEADED WITH EMMA...
WE MUST KEEP PETER'S MEMORY ALIVE IN RUSSIA - I CAN'T FIGHT THE BUREAUCRATS ALONE!
... MORE AND MORE I AM COMING TO THE CONCLUSION WE CAN DO NOTHING HERE.
THE SOVIETS USED MAKNO'S MILITIA AGAINST WHITE GENERAL WRANGEL THEN TURNED AND WIPED OUT THE FREE PEASANT LEADERS.
BUT NESTOR MAKNO ESCAPED TO DRINK HIMSELF TO DEATH IN PARIS...
EMMA AND SASHA WERE SHADOWED BY U.S. AS WELL AS SOVIET AGENTS. ONE POSED AS AN AP REPORTER. NO U.S. ALLY COULD ISSUE THEM TRAVEL PERMITS. ALL THEIR MAIL WAS READ BY THE STATE DEPARTMENT. BUT EMMA'S FAMILY MANAGED TO GET SOME MONEY THROUGH, AND SHE TRADED FOR FOOD AT THE OPEN MARKET.
THE CZAR'S OWN CREST!! SURELY THAT'S WORTH MORE THAN THREE POTATOS!
© Sharon Rudahl 07

SYMPATHETIC GUESTS OF THE YOUNG SOVIET UNION WERE SPOON FED GOOD NEWS AND GUIDED TO SUNNY SCENES. IWW BIG BILL HAYWOOD JUMPED BAIL TO JOIN THE REVOLUTION.
RUSSIA! HOME OF THE LIBERATED PROLETARIAT!!
SOVIET RUSSIA HAS BECOME A SOCIALIST LOURDES, A HOLY PLACE WHERE THE GULLIBLE COME TO SEE STAGED MIRACLES...
COMRADES IN WEIMAR GERMANY INVITED SASHA AND EMMA TO AN ANARCHIST CONVENTION...
I'M APPLYING FOR MY VISA AS "MISS E.G. KERSNER"— WHO DO YOU WANT TO BE?
THE RUSSIAN REVOLUTION WAS DEAD LONG AGO...
... I MET A SMUGGLER WHO SAYS HE CAN GET ME OUT TO TALINN, ESTONIA...
PASSPORTS ARRIVED BEFORE THE SMUGGLER'S ICE BOAT. DECEMBER 1921— AFTER TWO YEARS OF DISILLUSIONMENT, EMMA AND SASHA LEFT THEIR NATIVE LAND FOR THE LAST TIME.
ALL MY LIFE, I FED ON THE WONDERFUL SPIRIT OF RUSSIA... ALL MY LIFE I LONGED TO SEE IT SET FREE...
... MY DREAMS CRUSHED, MY FAITH BROKEN, MY HEART LIKE A STONE....
©Sharon Rudahl

To the BARRICADES
SEIZE THE BOLSHEVIK SPIES!!
WE'RE SENDING YOU BACK TO YOUR OWN COUNTRY!!
EMMA AND SASHA LEFT RUSSIA WITH FELLOW BUFORD DEPORTEE ALEXANDER SHAPIRO. JUST ACROSS THE LATVIAN BORDER, LOCAL POLICE HAULED THEM OFF THE TRAIN.
BUT WE DON'T HAVE A COUNTRY!
EMMA ASSUMED THEY HAD BEEN TRICKED BY THE SOVIETS. IN FACT, U.S. STATE DEPARTMENT AGENTS WANTED TIME TO SEARCH THEIR BAGGAGE...
YOUR PASSPORTS ARE IN ORDER... BUT I'M AFRAID NO ONE CAN SIGN FOR YOUR RELEASE UNTIL AFTER THE CHRISTMAS HOLIDAYS!
PASSPORT
LET ME KNOW WHEN YOU'RE DONE WITH THE WARDEN'S GAS RING...
MY SAILOR GIRL CAN WHIP UP A FEAST ANYWHERE!
THAT'S OKAY... IF JESUS WERE ON EARTH NOW HE WOULD SURELY BE IN JAIL.
THE KINDLY LATVIAN GUARD OFFERED TO GO SHOPPING FOR THEM, BRINGING BACK FRUIT, HONEY, NUTS, COFFEE, TINNED MILK AND FISH, BREAD AND CHEESE.
JANUARY 2 1922 – THE FREED PRISONERS REACHED STOCKHOLM, SWEDEN.
POST RESTANTE
ANY MAIL FOR MISS KERSNER??
INGETING!
IF WE DON'T GET VISAS SOON THEY REALLY WILL SEND US BACK TO RUSSIA!
I SHALL LEAVE WITHOUT NOTICE AND ENTER WITHOUT PERMISSION.
A SWEDISH WORKERS' PUBLICATION SENT FORMER IWW SEAMAN ARTUR SWENSSON TO BE THEIR TRANSLATOR.
I PICK UP PLENTY ENGLISH ON DOCKS!
©Sharon Rudahl '07

ARTUR WAS 29 YEARS OLD TO EMMA'S 53...
NEVER THINK I MEET THE GREAT EMMA GOLDMAN!
SHE BEGAN A TORRID LOVE AFFAIR WITH THE HANDSOME SWEDE...
SASHA STOWED AWAY TO GERMANY ON A TRAMP STEAMER. WITH ARTUR'S HELP, EMMA TRIED TO FOLLOW...
LIE FLAT, COVER WITH BLANKET-GUARD MAKES HIS ROUND!
HOUNDED BY U.S. AND SOVIET AGENTS, REJECTED BY FORMER COMRADES FOR HER ANTI-BOLSHEVISM, AMID THE RUIN OF LIFE-LONG HOPES, WHAT COULD EMMA DO ???
WHAT ARE YOU UP TO?? WE'LL FIND OUT AT THE GUARDHOUSE!!
PLEASE, SIR, WE HAD NO PLACE TO BE ALONE TOGETHER...
KRONER
WELL... BE OFF WITH YOU... BUT DON'T TRY IT AGAIN!!
THE GERMAN CONSUL GRANTED EMMA A 10 DAY VISA. IN APRIL 1922 SHE JOINED SASHA IN BERLIN.
... A FEW OF THE OLD MOTHER EARTH CREW ARE IN TOWN... THE ROCKERS ARE THROWING YOU A WELCOME BANQUET... YOU WON'T BELIEVE WHAT'S GOING ON IN THE THEATERS...
BERLIN
WEIMAR GERMANY! A BRIEF LIBERAL DEMOCRACY CRUSHED BY WORLD WAR I REPARATIONS. LURID FLOWERING OF SICKLY FREEDOMS, RUINOUS INFLATION AND SULLEN HUMILIATION, SEEDBED OF HITLER'S THIRD REICH.
© Sharon Rudahl '07

EMMA OVERSTAYED HER GERMAN VISA BY MORE THAN 2 YEARS, WRITING AND LECTURING IN LEFT-WING SOCIETY. ARTUR SENT LOVE LETTERS AND THEN TRAVELED TO BERLIN ON FALSE PAPERS.
WE ALL NEED LOVE AND UNDERSTANDING... AND A WOMAN NEEDS A DAMN SIGHT MORE WHEN SHE GROWS OLDER...
BUT AFTER A FEW MONTHS HE LEFT FOR AMERICA WITH EMMA'S YOUNG SECRETARY.
YOU WILL ALWAYS BE MY INSPIRATION!
SASHA MET 22 YEAR OLD EMMY ECSTEIN ON THE TERRACE OF A BERLIN CAFE. HER WELL-TO-DO JEWISH FAMILY DISAPPROVED. BUT EMMY WOULD DEVOTE THE REST OF HER SHORT, PAIN-FILLED LIFE TO HIM...
EMMY UNDERSTANDS HOW IMPORTANT OUR FRIENDSHIP WILL ALWAYS BE TO ME..
SOME LUCK THAT OLD LOBSTER HAS!
BUT I DO NEED YOUR RECIPE FOR BLINTZES.
HOW CAN YOU ATTACK REVOLUTION IN THE CAPITALIST PRESS?!
New York World
CONTRACT
AUTHOR
WILL
18 MO
EMMA'S REPORTS ON SOVIET RUSSIA WERE REJECTED BY LIBERAL PUBLICATIONS. STELLA RELAYED AN OFFER FROM THE MASS MARKET NEW YORK WORLD.
©Sharon Rudahl '07
I MUST BE HEARD, EVEN IF IT IS FOR THE LAST TIME.
I AM ACCUSED OF HAVING BETRAYED MY PAST BY PEOPLE WITH NO PAST TO BETRAY...
didn't get soft job you expected in Russia
Comrade!!! sold out the revolution to make big bucks
OLD FRIENDS CAME TO GERMANY FOR EMMA'S 54TH BIRTHDAY PARTY: FITZI FROM MOTHER EARTH, ANARCHIST DEPORTEE MOLLY STEIMER, STELLA AND HER SON IAN.
SUCH A JOY TO BE WITH YOU AGAIN TANTE EMMA
...BUT I'M AFRAID I CAN'T BE MUCH HELP— THE DOCTORS SAY I'M GOING BLIND...
HER SEVEN ARTICLES WERE EXPANDED INTO THE BOOK MY DISILLUSIONMENT IN RUSSIA
GERMAN EYE-DOCTORS ARE THE WORLD'S BEST—WE'LL FIND SOMEONE WHO CAN CURE YOU!!

COUNT WISER'S EXPERIMENTAL EYE EXERCISES DID SAVE STELLA'S SIGHT. TO CELEBRATE EMMA AND FRIENDS PLANNED AN EXCURSION TO THE MUNICH WAGNER FESTIVAL...
HALT! POLIZEI!
BITTE, YOUR PAPERS!
BAVARIAN POLICE...
I'M AFRAID WE'LL HAVE TO RETURN TO BERLIN WITHOUT PAYING OUR RESPECTS TO HERR WAGNER!
HA
HA
HA
WHEN WE TAKE OVER WE'LL FIX YOUR KIND!
VERDAMNTE JUDEN!!
LIKE WE DID ROSA LUXEMBURG!
EMMA HAD LONG BEEN PEN PALS WITH FRANK HARRIS, IRISH AUTHOR OF THE SEXUALLY EXPLICIT MY LIFE AND LOVES. THE TWO OLD OUTLAWS MET IN PARIS, WHERE FRANK WAS AVOIDING PROSECUTION ON OBSCENITY CHARGES...
ENGLAND IS THE SAFEST PLACE FOR YOU, DARLING. I HAVE FRIENDS IN THE LABOR GOVERNMENT—
©Sharon Rudahl '07
BUT WE MUST GET YOU SORTED OUT BEFORE THE TORIES TAKE OVER...
AT 68, AFTER AN ELABORATE DINNER AND ENOUGH WINE TO DROP MOST MEN, FRANK COULD STILL RUN 12 BLOCKS...
UTAMOH
ERANO
JULY 1924 - EMMA MOVED TO LONDON.
I DREADED ENGLAND'S BLEAKNESS AND FOGS. I HAD BEEN IN ARCHANGEL WHEN THE TEMPERATURE WAS 50° BELOW AND NOT FELT SO CHILLY!

THE RADICAL BRITISH ELITE TREATED EMMA TO BANQUETS ATTENDED BY BERTRAND RUSSELL, H. G. WELLS, REBECCA WEST AND EXPAT ERNEST HEMINGWAY.
WE OF THE BRITISH LABOR MISSION SPENT 6 ENTIRE WEEKS IN RUSSIA AND SAW NO REPRESSION!?!
WHAT ARE YOUR PLANS FOR ENGLAND, MISS GOLDMAN?
IF I CAN ROUSE OPINION AGAINST THE BOLSHEVIKS, IT MIGHT CURB EXECUTIONS IN THE CHEKA CELLARS!
BUT LOOK WHAT RUSSIA HAS ACHIEVED—
ART FOR THE MASSES—
CONCERTS, CHESS AND THEATER IN THE FACTORIES—
ABOLISHING THE ANTI-HOMOSEXUAL LAW—
I WONDER WHAT YOU LABOR MPs WOULD SAY IF SCOTLAND YARD SHOT WORKERS FOR GOING ON STRIKE!?!
THE FAMILY CODE OF 1918, GIVING WOMEN PROPERTY RIGHTS...
...FREEDOM TO CHOOSE THEIR HUSBANDS, THE RIGHT TO DIVORCE, LEGALIZING ABORTION...
PUBLIC EDUCATION, LITERACY FOR ALL...
SOCIALIZED MEDICINE, SANITATION, PROGRESS AGAINST ANCIENT PLAGUES...
THE END OF CHILD LABOR—
POLITICAL PRISONERS, THOUGHT CONTROL, MASS EXPULSIONS, FAMINE, DICTATORSHIP, FORCED LABOR, CENSORSHIP, PERSECUTIONS, POLICE STATE!
©Sharon Rudahl '07
THE REAL REBIRTH OF SOCIETY MUST BE BASED ON JUSTICE AND EQUALITY, THE LOVE OF LIBERTY AND OF HUMAN BROTHERHOOD!
ARCH REBEL EMMA GOLDMAN ALLIED WITH THE TORIES AGAINST THE WORKERS' REPUBLIC!?!
FREE SOVIET PRISONERS
YOU ARE LOATHE TO LET GO OF THE REVOLUTION IN TERMS OF DESTRUCTION AND TERROR— AND I AM DONE WITH THAT FOR ALL TIME...
VERY MUCH OBLIGED!
DON'T MENTION IT, COMRADE.
EMMA GAVE SPEECHES IN FOG AND SLEET ALL OVER BRITAIN. 1926— TO SECURE PAPERS, SHE ACCEPTED MARRIAGE TO 65 YEAR OLD WELSH MINER AND ANARCHIST JAMES COLTON.

IN LONDON EMMA OCCUPIED HERSELF DOING RESEARCH FOR A LECTURE SERIES ON RUSSIAN THEATER...
EMMA GIVES ME THE FEELING SOMEONE EXISTS WHOSE LOVE REALLY EMBRACES ALL HUMANITY!
LONDONERS ARE ABOUT THE LAST WORD IN SUPPRESSION OF EMOTION!
SHE MADE INTRODUCTIONS AND BOOKED CONCERTS FOR A FELLOW POLITICAL EXILE, THE GREAT AFRICAN AMERICAN SINGER PAUL ROBESON.
MAY 1926 — ON THE 10TH DAY OF BRITAIN'S GREAT GENERAL STRIKE EMMA LEFT ENGLAND FOR FRANCE.
...IT SEEMS I AM A TURNCOAT AND CAN'T BE TRUSTED EVEN TO WRITE A MANIFESTO! HOW COULD I REMAIN IN ENGLAND??
HEIRESS AND ART COLLECTOR PEGGY GUGGENHEIM BOUGHT EMMA "A LITTLE VILLA OF 3 ROOMS" IN THE THEN SLEEPY FISHING VILLAGE OF ST. TROPEZ.
EMMA, IT'S TIME YOU TOLD YOUR OWN STORY, THE WHOLE BACKGROUND OF YOUR LIFE AND WORK —
AH, BUT THAT WOULD MEAN THE RESURRECTION OF MEMORIES I DO NOT WISH TO DIG OUT...
THE NEXT YEAR EMMA USED HER PASSPORT AS COLTON'S WIFE TO TOUR CANADA. SHE GAVE DRAMA LECTURES AND RAISED FUNDS FOR FALSELY CONVICTED ANARCHISTS SACCO AND VANZETTI.
"PERMISSION TO ENTER THE UNITED STATES DENIED." BUT LENA'S COMING TO TORONTO, AND THAT DELI OWNER WHO SENT YOU FOOD IN PRISON —
DR. BEN'S DROPPING BY ON HIS WAY TO A MEDICAL CONFERENCE — HE'S BECOME A RESPECTED AUTHORITY ON VENEREAL DISEASE!!
1928 — AFTER THE EXECUTIONS OF SACCO AND VANZETTI EMMA RETURNED TO ST. TROPEZ AND BEGAN WRITING HER AUTOBIOGRAPHY.
IN ALL MY YEARS IN EUROPE I NEVER FELT SO VITAL AND ALIVE AS I DID IN THE STATES...
ALL OUR ARCHIVES WERE SEIZED IN THE RAIDS ON MOTHER EARTH. BUT I ASKED OLD FRIENDS TO SEND BACK LETTERS, AND RECEIVED 1000'S!
Emma
500 FROM BEN REITMAN, ALONE!
© Sharon Rudahl '07

PEGGY GUGGENHEIM RAISED FUNDS TO PAY A TYPIST. SASHA OFFERED TO EDIT. HE SETTLED WITH EMMY ECSTEIN IN NEARBY ST. CLOUD.
AM I OVER-EMPHASIZING MY SEX LIFE?
IN YOUR LIFE, YOUR LOVE LIFE WAS OF AN EMPHATIC NATURE, AND IT IS ALSO EMPHASIZED IN YOUR BOOK.
BERLIN LEFTIST RUDOLF ROCKER WAS ONE OF THE SUMMER HOUSE GUESTS AT ST. TROPEZ:
EMMA GOT UP AT 6, MADE COFFEE AND WROTE FOR SEVERAL HOURS...
...THEN SHE CLEANED HOUSE, WROTE,...
...MADE LUNCH...
...WROTE... MADE DINNER...
...IN THE EVENING, SHE KEPT UP HER CORRESPONDENCE...
EMMA GOLDMAN'S 1000 PAGE LIVING MY LIFE WAS PUBLISHED IN 1931 TO MOSTLY FAVORABLE REVIEWS...
The New York Times
Her heart is alright whatever may be said of her dogma....
HERALD TRIBUNE
A Great Woman's story of a brave adventure...
The New Republic
Total lack of ideology...
THE GREAT DEPRESSION GRIPPED THE U.S.. IN EUROPE HARD TIMES FUELED THE RISE OF FASCIST TYRANTS PROMISING EASY ANSWERS. EMMA TOURED WARNING AGAINST ADOLF HITLER TWO YEARS BEFORE HIS ELECTION AS GERMAN CHANCELLOR.
DICTATORSHIP WORLD MENACE
TONITE EMMA GOLDMAN
DIRTY JEWS!!
NOTABLES INCLUDING SINCLAIR LEWIS AND JOSEPHINE BAKER URGED THE U.S. GOVERNMENT TO GRANT EMMA A VISA. SHE WAS ALLOWED 90 DAYS TO GIVE DRAMA LECTURES.
TONIGHT WE HAVE TRACED THE ROOTS OF THE GERMAN TRAGEDY FRIDAY'S LECTURE WILL EXPLORE THE COLLAPSE OF GERMAN CULTURE
ELDERLY RED HERE TO PAY US A VISIT
EMMA WAS EXPLICITLY FORBIDDEN TO GIVE HER ANTI-HITLER SPEECH. BUT AS ALWAYS, SHE SAID WHAT SHE HAD COME TO SAY...
©Sharon Rudahl '07

F.B.I. DIRECTOR J. EDGAR HOOVER KEPT A CLOSE EYE ON EMMA. BUT TO MOST AMERICANS SHE WAS A HARMLESS CURIOSITY FROM ANOTHER ERA. HER COMMERCIAL MANAGER FAILED TO FILL LARGE HIGH-RENT HALLS...
NOT MUCH OF A COMEBACK, STELLA...
...MY VISA'S UP AND WE HAVEN'T CLEARED ENOUGH TO PAY PASSAGE BACK TO ST. TROPEZ!
IS THERE ENOUGH FOR A TRAIN TICKET TO TORONTO? JEWISH COMRADES BEG YOU TO GIVE ANTI-FASCISM TALKS IN CANADA...
IN TORONTO THAT SUMMER OF 1934, EMMA HAD HER LAST ROMANTIC ADVENTURE, WITH BLIND SOCIOLOGIST FRANK HEINER.
YOU ARE LIFE, YOU ARE ETERNITY...
EMMA WAS 64, FRANK 36. SHE FULFILLED EVERY WOMAN'S SECRET WISH – TO BE PASSIONATELY LOVED FOR WHAT CANNOT BE SEEN IN HER MIRROR.
"TWO FASCINATING, OVERPOWERING, ECSTATIC WEEKS – I AM INFATUATED AS ONLY OLD FOOLS CAN BE..." ♡ Emma
Sasha
"I AM DAMN GLAD YOU WILL SOON BE WITH ME – NO, NOT ONLY THE BLINTZES AND GEFILTE FISH!"
I DON'T THINK YOU HAVE ANYTHING TO REGRET BUT IT IS A HOPELESS SITUATION...
FEDYA SENT A CABLE TO TORONTO WARNING EMMA THAT SASHA'S HEALTH WAS FAILING. FRIENDS PASSED THE HAT TO PAY HER WAY BACK TO FRANCE.
© Sharon Rudahl '07
SASHA FACED A SECOND OPERATION FOR PROSTATE CANCER. HIS COMPANION EMMY ECSTEIN WAS ALSO CRITICALLY ILL.
I HAVE LIVED MY LIFE... WHEN ONE HAS NEITHER HEALTH NOR MEANS AND CANNOT WORK FOR HIS IDEALS IT IS TIME TO CLEAR OUT...
NO ONE ELSE WAS EVER SO ROOTED IN EVERY FIBER OF MY BEING...

JUNE 27 1936 – AFTER FIRST SENDING EMMA A BIRTHDAY TELEGRAM, SASHA BERKMAN SHOT HIMSELF –
EMMY ECSTEIN REACHED EMMA VIA A NEIGHBOR'S PHONE. EMMA HAD TO WAIT 3½ HOURS FOR THE BUS FROM ST. TROPEZ TO ST. CLOUD...
TAKE THIS DOWN, EMMY... NO, YOU MUSTN'T GET HYSTERICAL..."I, ALEXANDER BERKMAN, TESTIFY THAT I SHOT MYSELF. NO ONE ELSE IS RESPONSIBLE"... GIVE IT TO ME TO SIGN NOW, DEAR...
WHEN SHE ARRIVED SASHA WAS STILL CONSCIOUS –
DEAREST SAILOR MINE, STAUNCHEST CHUM OF MY LIFETIME.....
OUR FRIENDSHIP IS THE ONE TREASURE I HAVE RESCUED FROM MY LONG AND BITTER STRUGGLE...
THE LARGEST PART OF MY LIFE FOLLOWED OUR COMRADE TO THE GRAVE...
BEFORE DYING, SASHA ASKED EMMA TO LOOK AFTER EMMY ECSTEIN...
...AND EMMA MADE AN ALLOWANCE OUT OF HER OWN LIMITED FUNDS FOR THE FEW YEARS THAT EMMY LINGERED...
© Sharon Rudahl '07

SPAIN

SPAIN HAD A FIERY TRADITION OF **STRUGGLE.** WHILE 1920'S DICTATOR PRIMO DE RIVERA PURSUED A **RUINOUS** COLONIAL WAR IN MOROCCO, HIRED GUNMEN ASSASSINATED **UNION LEADERS.** ANARCHISTS FIELDED THEIR **OWN** PISTOLEROS. WIDESPREAD **UNREST** INCLUDED AN ANARCHIST **UPRISING** AT CASAS VIEJAS AND A **MINERS' REVOLT** IN HISTURIAS. BRUTAL **RIGHT-WING** REPRESSION **FOLLOWED**, ENCOURAGED BY A FEARFUL AND **REACTIONARY CATHOLIC CHURCH.**

IN 1936, AFTER A MERE 5 YEARS OF REPRESENTATIVE GOVERNMENT, SPANISH CITIZENS ELECTED A FRAGILE LEFT-LIBERAL COALITION... TWO MONTHS AFTER SASHA'S **DEATH**, EMMA GOLDMAN WAS CALLED **TO THE BARRICADES!**

JULY 1936- FASCIST GENERAL FRANCISCO FRANCO LED AN ARMY REVOLT AGAINST THE ELECTED GOVERNMENT-
... MILITARY COUP OVERTHROWS SPANISH REPUBLIC - ANARCHIST MILITIAS HOLD REGION OF CATALONIA-
A CABLE, MME. GOLDMAN- FROM SPAIN!!
EMMA AWOKE FROM MOURNING...
WESTERN UNION
SPANISH WORKER ANARCHIST FEDERATION REQUEST EMMA GOLDMAN DIRECT ENGLISH LANGUAGE PRESS BUREAU PLEASE REPLY CNT/FAI
I WILL BE ON THE SCENE OF REVOLUTIONARY ACTION!! I WILL LIVE UP TO SASHA'S SPIRIT!
AT AGE SIXTY-SEVEN, SHE SECRETLY CROSSED THE BORDER INTO SPAIN...
COMRADE...
ESPAGNE
FRANCE
REPUBLICAN CATALONIA! SHOPS, RESTAURANTS, TRANSPORT, HOSPITALS, FARMS AND FACTORIES OPERATE SMOOTHLY AS WORKERS' CO-OPS. THE STREETS OF BARCELONA FILL WITH EAGER VOLUNTEERS SINGING REVOLUTIONARY SONGS...
COLECTIVIZIDAD
BARBERIA
P.O.U.M.
OBRERO SINDICATO
VIVA
U.G.T.
INDUSTRIA GASTRONOMICA COL
ABRAHAM LINCOLN BRIGADE
FAI
viva la revolucia
CNT
CNT FAI
SOLIDARIDAD
©Sharon Rudahl '07
GEORGE ORWELL
"WAITERS AND SHOP WALKERS LOOKED YOU IN THE FACE AND TREATED YOU AS AN EQUAL... NOBODY SAID 'SEÑOR', EVERYBODY CALLED EVERYBODY ELSE 'COMRADE'."

EMMA VISITED COLLECTIVIZED RAILROADS, GAS WORKS AND FACTORIES, ADDRESSED MASS MEETINGS AND DELIVERED ENGLISH LANGUAGE BROADCASTS.
...YOU MUST MAKE READY TO FIGHT ON EVERY FRONT THAT THREATENS THE LIBERTY OF SPAIN!!!
THE FASCIST DANGER HAS TO BE MET ALMOST WITH BARE HANDS!
WESTERN DEMOCRACIES TOOK A STAND OF "MALEVOLENT NEUTRALITY" TOWARD THE SPANISH REPUBLIC, NOT EVEN PERMITTING ARMS SALES.
...THIS IS THE BBC... IN SPAIN, CHURCH-BURNING REDS CONTINUE TO LOSE GROUND..
SHE GREETED MILITIAS ON THE FRONT AT ARAGON, AND CONFERRED WITH BUENAVENTURA DURRUTI IN THE TRENCHES OUTSIDE MADRID.
YOU WOULD THINK THE REPUBLICANS WERE THE REBELS AND FRANCO THE DEFENDER OF DEMOCRACY!!
3,200 U.S. IDEALISTS FOUGHT IN ABRAHAM LINCOLN BRIGADES. BRITISH LABOR RAISED HUMANITARIAN AID. BUT ONLY THE SOVIET UNION SENT TRAINED ADVISORS, AIRPLANES AND WEAPONS.
NAZI GERMANY AND MUSSOLINI'S ITALY RUSHED ADVANCED ARMS TO COUNTER THE SOVIET UNION... SPAIN BECAME THE TEST SITE FOR WORLD WAR II.
THE TRAGIC MAY DAYS OF 1937— REPUBLICAN TROOPS FIRED ON ANARCHISTS. CNT-FAI LEADERS WERE EXECUTED, 1000'S ARRESTED, COLLECTIVES SMASHED... EMMA RETURNED TO LONDON TO CLOSE DOWN THE CNT-FAI PRESS OFFICE.
MUJERES LIBRES
THE POPULAR FRONT IS OFFERING 4 MINISTRIES TO THE ANARCHISTS...
I FEAR THE COMMUNISTS WILL SELL US OUT!
COMRADE STALIN DECIDED YOU NEED A DISCIPLINED ARMY- WE WILL DISBAND THESE VOLUNTEERS.
IF WE CAN'T UNITE AMONG OURSELVES, HOW CAN WE CALL ON THE WORKERS OF THE WORLD?!?
LONDON OBSERVER
REDS ROUTED FRANCO NEAR MADRID
© Sharon Rudahl '07
IN SPAIN THE LAST RESISTANCE CRUMBLED. REFUGEES FLED.
AS FRANCO ENTERED ABANDONED BARCELONA, EMMA SORTED PAPERS FOR A DUTCH EXHIBIT ON ALEXANDER BERKMAN.
I MISS SASHA MORE SINCE THE SPANISH STRUGGLE AND DEFEAT...
THE PLAGUE OF FASCISM SPREAD ACROSS EUROPE... HITLER OCCUPIED AUSTRIA AND CZECHOSLOVAKIA.
AID FOR SPANISH REFUGEES
ONE COUNTRY COULD NOT FIGHT AGAINST THE ENTIRE WORLD!

MARCH 1939 ~ EMMA LEFT EUROPE FOR CANADA...
I KNOW NOW THAT I WILL BE AN ALIEN ABROAD FOR THE REST OF MY LIFE...
IN TORONTO EMMA RAISED FUNDS FOR THE FIGHT AGAINST FASCISM AND AID FOR ITS VICTIMS. SPEAKING IN ENGLISH AND YIDDISH, SHE DEMANDED THE RIGHT OF ASYLUM FOR JEWISH REFUGEES FLEEING HITLER - INCLUDING IN BRITISH PALESTINE.
שלום
SO MANY TELEGRAMS FROM OVERSEAS!
"MAY YOU LIVE 10,000 YEARS" — FROM REVOLUTIONARY CHINESE WRITER BA JIN!!
HERE'S ONE FROM THE CNT-FAI LEADER...
EMMA CELEBRATED HER 70TH BIRTHDAY IN CANADA WITH STELLA AND MANY OLD FRIENDS...
"THE SPANISH MILITANTS ADMIRE AND REVERE YOU... WE DECLARE YOU OUR SPIRITUAL MOTHER..."
MARIANO VASQUEZ
EMMA'S LAST CAMPAIGN WAS TO SAVE FOUR YOUNG ITALIAN-CANADIANS FROM DEPORTATION UNDER THE WAR MEASURES ACT.
SAVE ARTHUR BORTOLOTTI
...AND WHAT WAS HIS CRIME?!? POSSESSING AN ANTI-FASCIST LEAFLET!! IF BORTOLOTTI IS SENT BACK TO ITALY HE WILL BE MURDERED BY MUSSOLINI'S BLACK SHIRTS!
AFTER BORTOLOTTI WAS RELEASED FROM PRISON SICK WITH FLU, EMMA VISITED HIS ROOMING HOUSE DAILY.
A BISSEL CHICKEN SOUP...
FEBRUARY 17, 1940 - EMMA WAS WAITING FOR BORTOLOTTI TO GIVE HER AND OTHER COMRADES A RIDE TO AN ANTI-FASCIST MEETING...
EMMA?!? WHAT'S THE MATTER!?
QUICK— CALL AN AMBULANCE!!
©Sharon Rudahl '07
AS SHE WAS CARRIED ON THE STRETCHER, EMMA REACHED TO TUG DOWN HER SKIRT TO COVER HER KNEES...

EMMA HAD SUFFERED A STROKE. HER NIECE STELLA STAYED BESIDE HER UNTIL THE END.
SHE DIED MAY 14, 1940.
"I HAD DRUNK THE CUP TO THE LAST DROP..."
EMMA'S BODY WAS ALLOWED TO CROSS THE U.S. BORDER. SHE WAS BURIED AT WALDHEIM CEMETARY IN CHICAGO, NEAR THE HAYMARKET MARTYRS...
A VETERAN OF THE ORLENOFF THEATER TROUPE READ THE GRAVEYARD SCENE FROM HAMLET...
"ALAS, POOR YORICK..."
STELLA PLACED MATCHING BOUQUETS OF SPRING FLOWERS ON EMMA'S AND VOLTAIRINE'S GRAVES...
DR. BEN REITMAN PUT RED ROSES INTO THE ARMS OF THE HAYMARKET MEMORIAL.
© Sharon Rudahl '07

IN 1934, WHEN EMMA GOLDMAN WAS 65, HARPER'S MAGAZINE ASSIGNED HER AND OTHER **CELEBRITIES** THE TOPIC: "WAS MY LIFE WORTH LIVING?"

"WHAT IS GENERALLY REGARDED AS SUCCESS - ACQUISITION OF WEALTH, THE CAPTURE OF POWER OR SOCIAL PRESTIGE - I CONSIDER THE MOST DISMAL FAILURES...
IF I HAD MY LIFE TO LIVE OVER AGAIN, LIKE ANYONE ELSE I SHOULD WISH TO ALTER MINOR DETAILS.
BUT IN ANY OF MY MORE IMPORTANT ACTIONS AND ATTITUDES I WOULD REPEAT MY LIFE AS I HAVE LIVED IT."

THROUGHOUT HER MORE THAN HALF A CENTURY OF FEARLESS TROUBLE-MAKING, EMMA'S VOICE COULD NOT BE STIFLED. ONCE HEARD, SHE COULD NOT BE FORGOTTEN...MAY WE REMEMBER HER TODAY.

Sharon Rudahl MARCH '07

AUTHOR'S NOTE

Almost everything you have just read Emma Goldman and her friends say or think was taken directly from their own essays or speeches or was quoted in Emma's thousand-page autobiography, *Living My Life*. I did take some liberties editing for brevity or context and made up minor dialogue to move plot along. The most glaring example: there was a real social broken up by the police, probably at Ben Reitman's invitation. But Tillie the barmaid and her conversations with Emma must be credited to the artist's imagination.

Special thanks are due to Dr. Alice Wexler for generously allowing me free run of her lifetime of Emma Goldman scholarship. Thanks also to my patient and sympathetic editors Paul Buhle and Sarah Fan. Paul was the instigator of this project and refused to give in to my self-doubts. Thanks also to Jack Peters and Jesse Peters for invaluable computer assistance.

I was born in 1947 near Washington, D.C., and grew up in a suburban ghetto of second- and third-generation Russian Jewish immigrants whose parents or grandparents had been part of Emma's wave of immigration. My own grandmother's parents did not think she needed an education. She stole a fish from the kitchen and took it to the rabbi in the next village, begging to be taught to read. My first political confrontation was with my junior high school principal. I demanded that our traditional "Christmas Program" include some token reference to Chanukah. He threatened to expel me, but I stood my ground. There was nothing I longed for so much as getting out of that school. So at age thirteen, I made the invaluable discovery that anyone can be powerful if they are indifferent to consequences. We had one of the first "Holiday Programs" complete with singing dreidels.

The next year, I took the bus to the Kennedy White House to join Ban the Bomb marchers, the first demonstrations since the executions of the Rosenbergs. Childhood outrage at the "White" and "Negro" signs on the Union Train Station water fountains—the first sparkling clean, the second dirty and corroded—impelled me to join early D.C.-area civil rights marches. These were not the peaceful love feasts of the "I Have a Dream" climax of that movement but little-reported demonstrations often violently broken up by all-white capital police. Children and women marched singing at the front, hoping to slow the attack. For my generation, the murders of civil rights "Freedom Riders" James Chaney, Andrew Goodman, and Michael Schwerner had the same galvanizing effect as the Haymarket executions for Emma and her peers.

I kept marching in demonstrations against U.S. military intervention in Indochina, gatherings of a few score hardcore dissenters that swelled into the movement against the Vietnam War. Students home from universities in California seeded cultural and political ferment. The times were changing and for a while those who marched to a different drummer felt they were followed by a vast parade.

As an art student on scholarship in New York City, I lived a few blocks from Emma's old digs in a tenement on East Thirteenth Street and took classes at the Peter Cooper Foundation Building, where she had orated for free speech. Buildings in my neighborhood still had faded signs for Yiddish theater. But my generation was exploring new social and sexual possibilities, the liberation so essential to Emma's vision. Ah, if only I could have invited Emma to certain be-ins in the park, to certain nights in the streets, she might almost have believed her dreams had come to life.

After art school, I worked on antiwar underground newspapers in Madison, Wisconsin, and San Francisco, California. In the early 1970s, I contributed to and edited issues of the feminist *Wimmen's Comix.* Jailed after one antiwar demonstration with other members of the Good Times Newspaper Collective, I made the same discovery Emma had about my fellow inmates: their chief crimes seemed to be ignorance and poverty. One had stolen a wig, one in desperation passed a bad check, the gentle old trustee had defended her kids against an abusive husband.

The Vietnam War ended, the underground newspapers folded, the world moved on. Less tenacious than Emma, I tried life in Tito's socialist Yugoslavia, traveling with a chess grandmaster, and returned to California to marry a different professional chess master. My political beliefs never altered, but family and work obligations kept me from doing much to advance them.

But as my sons grew up and completed home-schooling, I became more politically active again and ready to take risks. Recently jailed for writing "U.S. OUT OF IRAQ" on a utility box in West Hollywood, I recalled the songs from the civil rights era. I sang so loud and long in the lockup the station chief himself politely asked me: "Would you be willing to leave if we drop the charges?"

Here is a purported Jewish folk belief I read last summer in an ad for mortuary plots: God's throne is bejeweled with precious stones, each jewel manifesting a person who fulfilled his or her task in life. Though I am as resolute an atheist as Emma, for me her life is precisely such a jewel. How did Emma Goldman, indifferently educated, easily swayed by passion, rife with contradictions, nonetheless find her way clear through the thorniest issues of the twentieth century? I have no doubt Emma would effortlessly reject arguments for kidnapping, torturing, and indefinitely confining "enemies of freedom."

Emma never muddied her thirst for truth with chemical substitutes. She never willfully dimmed her inner light.

At different times, Emma Goldman has been appreciated for different aspects of her life and work: prescient rejecter of Soviet-style communism, free-spirited hippie dancer, icon of feminist pride. Let me add that, for my declining generation, Emma deserves special praise for completing the arc of her life with undiminished passion and integrity. Without compromise, without benefit of Botox, knee replacements, or 401(k) investments, she loved and fought until her end.

Learning about Emma and her colleagues gave me perspective on the outrages of our own day and comforted and encouraged me to never stop fighting or dancing. If these pages in any way encourage you to see more clearly and act more bravely, my work will have been well rewarded indeed.

—Sharon Rudahl

Printed in the USA
CPSIA information can be obtained
at www.ICGtesting.com
JSHW060042150824
68134JS00028B/2597